Common Desktop Environment 1.0
Advanced User's and System Administrator's Guide

CDE DOCUMENTATION GROUP

IBM • HEWLETT–PACKARD • SUNSOFT • NOVELL

Addison-Wesley Publishing Company

Reading, Massachusetts • Menlo Park, California • New York
Don Mills, Ontario • Wokingham, England • Amsterdam
Bonn • Sydney • Singapore • Tokyo • Madrid • San Juan
Paris • Seoul • Milan • Mexico City • Taipei

Library of Congress Cataloging-in-Publication Data

Common desktop environment 1.0. Advanced user's and system
administrator's guide/CDE Documentation Group.
p. cm. — (Common desktop environment 1.0 series)
Includes index.
ISBN 0-201-48952-X
1. Graphical user interfaces (Computer systems) 2. Common desktop
environment. 3. UNIX (Computer file) I. CDE Documentation Group.
II. Series.
QA76.9.U83C65 1995 95-11126
005.4'3—dc20 CIP

The CDE Documentation Group: Julia Blackmore, David Blomgren, Casey Cannon, Maria Cherem, Anna Ellendman, Janice Gelb, Mary Hamilton, Mindy Isham, David Jones, Astrid Julienne, Kathy McGovern, Don McMinds, Rob Patten, Janice Winsor, Doug Woestendiek

7 8 9 10 11 MA 00999897
Seventh printing, January 1997

Addison-Wesley books are available for bulk purchases by corporations, institutions, and other organizations. For more information please contact the Corporate, Government, and Special Sales Department at (800) 238-9682.

Contents

Preface

This manual covers advanced tasks in customizing the appearance and behavior of the Common Desktop Environment (CDE). It includes chapters on:

- Customizing system initialization, login, and session initiation
- Adding applications and providing interface representations for applications and their data
- Configuring desktop processes, applications, and data across the network
- Customizing desktop services such as window management, printing, colors, and fonts

Who Should Use This Book

The audiences for this book include:

- System administrators. Many of the tasks in this book require root permission.
- Advanced users who want to perform customizations that cannot be accomplished using the desktop user interface. The desktop provides user-specific locations for many of its configuration files.

How This Book Is Organized

This manual includes the following chapters:

Chapter 1, "Configuring Login Manager," covers how to configure the appearance and behavior of the desktop Login Manager.

Chapter 2, "Configuring Session Manager," covers how the desktop stores and retrieves sessions, and how to customize session startup.

Chapter 3, "Adding and Administering Applications," covers how Application Manager gathers applications, and explains how to add applications.

Chapter 4, "Registering an Application," covers how to create a registration package for an application.

Chapter 5, "Configuring the Desktop in a Network," covers how to distribute desktop services, applications, and data across a network.

Chapter 6, "Configuring and Administering Printing from the Desktop," covers how to add and remove desktop printers, and how to specify the default printer.

Chapter 7, "Desktop Search Paths," covers how the desktop finds applications, help files, icons, and other desktop data across the network.

Chapter 8, "Introduction to Actions and Data Types," introduces the concepts of actions and data types, and explains how they are used to provide a user interface for applications.

Chapter 9, "Creating Actions and Data Types Using Create Action," covers how to use the Create Action application to create actions and data types.

Chapter 10, "Creating Actions Manually," covers how to create action definitions by editing a database configuration file.

Chapter 11, "Creating Data Types Manually," covers how to create data type definitions by editing a database configuration file.

Chapter 12, "Creating Icons for the Desktop," covers how to use the Icon Editor, and naming conventions, sizes, and search paths for desktop icons.

Chapter 13, "Advanced Front Panel Customization," covers creating new system-wide controls and subpanels, and other panel customizations.

Chapter 14, "Customizing the Workspace Manager," covers customizing windows, mouse button bindings, keyboard bindings, and Workspace Manager menus.

Chapter 15, "Administering Application Resources, Fonts, and Colors," covers how to set application resources, and how the desktop uses fonts and colors.

Chapter 16, "Configuring Localized Desktop Sessions," covers system administration tasks for systems running international sessions.

What Typographic Changes and Symbols Mean

The following table describes the type changes and symbols used in this book.

Table P-1 Typographic Conventions

Typeface or Symbol	Meaning	Example
`AaBbCc123`	The names of commands, files, directories, and keywords.	Edit your `.dtprofile` file. Use `ls -a` to list all files.
AaBbCc123	Parameters or variables; replace with a real value	To delete a file, type `rm` *filename*.
AaBbCc123	Book titles, new words or terms, or words to be emphasized	Read Chapter 6 in *User's Guide*. These are called *class* options. You *must* be root to do this.

Configuring Login Manager 1

The Login Manager is a server responsible for displaying a login screen, authenticating users, and starting a user's session. The graphical login is an attractive alternative to the traditional character mode login for bitmap displays. Displays managed by the login server can be directly attached to the login server or attached to an X terminal or workstation on the network.

Note – You must be a root user to start, stop, or customize the login server.

The login server:

- Can display a login screen on bitmap displays unconditionally or by request on local and network bitmap displays
- Accommodates directly attached character console displays
- Can display a chooser screen that enables users to display login screens from other login servers on the network
- Allows controlled access to the login server
- Provides access to the traditional character-mode login

Displays managed by the Login Manager can be directly attached to the Login Manager server or attached to an X terminal or workstation on the network. For local displays, the login server will automatically start an X server and display a login screen. For network displays, such as X terminals, the login server supports the X Display Manager Protocol (XDMCP) 1.0, which allows displays to request that the login server display a login screen on the display.

Starting the Login Server

The login server is usually started when the system is booted. You can also start the login server from a command line.

- To set the login server to start when the system is booted, type `/usr/dt/bin/dtconfig -e`

  The login server will then start automatically when you reboot.

- To start the login server from a command line, type `/usr/dt/bin/dtlogin -daemon`

Note – Although starting the login server from the command line is available for temporary configuration testing, you should normally start the login server when the system is booted.

Managing Local and Network Displays

Figure 1-1 shows a possible login server configuration.

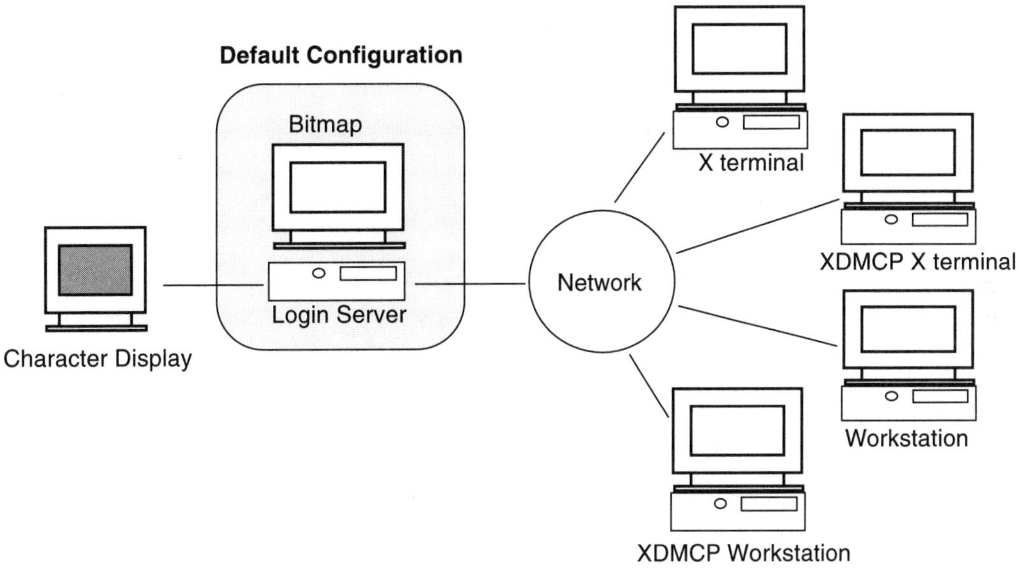

Figure 1-1 Possible login server configuration

Finding the Login Server Process ID

By default, the login server stores its process ID in `/var/dt/Xpid`.

To change this, you can set the `Dtlogin.pidFile` resource in the `Xconfig` file. If changed, the directory specified must exist when the login server is started.

To modify `Xconfig`, copy `Xconfig` from `/usr/dt/config` to `/etc/dt/config`. After modifying `/etc/dt/config/Xconfig`, tell the login server to reread `Xconfig` by typing:

```
/usr/dt/bin/dtconfig -reset
```

This issues the command `kill -HUP` *login server process ID.*

For example, to store the login server process ID in `/var/myservers/Dtpid`, set the following in the `Xconfig` file:

```
Dtlogin.pidFile: /var/myservers/Dtpid
```

When the login server is restarted, the login server will store its process ID in `/var/myservers/Dtpid`. The `/var/myservers` directory must exist when the login server is started.

Displaying a Login Screen on a Local Display

Upon startup, the login server checks the `Xservers` file to determine if an X server needs to be started and to determine if and how login screens should be displayed on local or network displays.

To modify `Xservers`, copy `Xservers` from `/usr/dt/config` to `/etc/dt/config`. After modifying `/etc/dt/config/Xservers`, tell the login server to reread `Xservers` by typing:

```
/usr/dt/bin/dtconfig -reset
```

This issues the command `kill -HUP` *login server process ID*

The format of an `Xservers` line is:

display_name display_class display_type X_server_command

where

display_name	Tells the login server the connection name to use when connecting to the X server (:0 in the following example). A value of * (asterisk) is expanded to *host name*:0. The number specified must match the number specified in the *X_server_command* connection number.
display_class	Identifies resources specific to this display (`Local` in the following example).
display_type	Tells the login server whether the display is local or a network display, and how to manage the Command Line Login option on the login screen (`local@console` in the following example).

X_server_command	Identifies the command line, connection number, and other options the login server will use to start the X server (`/usr/bin/X11/X: 0` in the following example). The connection number specified must match the number specified in the *display_name*.

The default `Xservers` line is similar to:

```
:0 Local local@console /usr/bin/X11/X :0
```

Running the Login Server without a Local Display

If your login server system has no bitmap display, run the login server without a local display by commenting out the `Xservers` line for the local display using a `#` (pound sign). For example,

```
# :0 Local local@console /usr/bin/X11/X :0
```

When the login server starts, it runs in the background waiting for requests from network displays.

Accessing Command Line Login on a Local Display

When the user selects Command Line Login on the login screen, the login server temporarily terminates the X server, allowing access to the traditional command-line login running on the bitmap display terminal device. After the user has logged in and then out, or after a specified time-out, the login server will restart the X server.

Note – The Command Line Login option is unavailable on network displays.

The *display_type* controls the behavior of Command Line Login. The format of *display_type* is:

- `local@`*display_ terminal_device*
- `local`
- `foreign`

When `local@`*display_terminal_device* is specified, the login server assumes that the X server and `/dev/`*display_terminal_device* are on the same physical device, and that a command line login (usually `getty`) is running on the device. When the user selects Command Line Login, the X server is terminated, allowing access to the running command-line login (`getty`) running on the `/dev/`*display_terminal_device*.

To disable the Command Line Login option on a display, specify `none` as the *display_terminal_device*. The default *display_terminal_device* is `console`. When `local` is specified, *display_terminal_device* defaults to `console`. When `foreign` is specified, Command Line Login is disabled.

Note – The Command Line Login option will be disabled on the local display when the login server is started from the command line.

Accommodating a Character Display Console

If your login server system has a directly attached character display serving as a console, you may also want to set *display_terminal_device* to `none` to disable Command Line Login on the bitmap display login screen.

Alternatively, if a command-line login (`getty`) is running on both the character display console and the bitmap display, you can change *display_terminal_device* to the command line login (`getty`) device on the bitmap display.

For example, if the bitmap display command-line login (`getty`) is on device `/dev/tty01`, change the *display_type* to `local@tty01`.

Displaying a Login Screen on a Network Display

The login server can accept requests from network displays to display a login screen on that particular display. The network display is usually an X terminal but can also be a workstation.

To manage requests from network displays, the login server supports the X Display Manager Protocol (XDMCP) 1.0. This protocol enables the login server to negotiate and accept or reject requests from network displays. Most X terminals have XDMCP built in.

XDMCP Direct Requests from Network Displays

When you configure your X terminal to use XDMCP direct (query mode), you tell your X terminal the host name of the login server host. When the X terminal is booted, it automatically contacts the login server, and the login server displays a login screen on the X terminal. See your X terminal documentation for information describing how to configure your X terminal for XDMCP direct mode.

Most X servers also support the `-query` option. In this mode, your X server behaves as if it were an X terminal, contacting the login server host directly and requesting that it display a login screen on the X server. For example, starting the X server on a bitmap display on workstation `bridget` will have login server `anita` display a login screen on the X server:

```
X -query anita
```

XDMCP Indirect Requests from Network Display

When you configure your X terminal to use XDMCP indirect mode, you tell your X terminal the host name of the login server host. When the X terminal is booted, it will contact the login server, and the login server will present a list, through a chooser screen, of other login server hosts on the network. From this list, the user can select a host, and that host will display a login screen on the user's X terminal. See your X terminal documentation for information describing how to configure your X terminal for XDMCP indirect mode.

As with direct mode, most X servers support the `-indirect` option, which causes your X server to contact the login server in XDMCP indirect mode.

Managing Non-XDMCP Network Displays

Older X terminals may not support XDMCP. For the login server to display a login screen on this type of X terminal, list the X terminal name in the `Xservers` file.

Example

The following lines in the `Xservers` file direct the login server to display a login screen on two non-XDMCP X terminals, `ruby` and `wolfie`:

```
ruby.blackdog.com:0 AcmeXsta foreign
```

```
wolfie:0 PandaCo foreign
```

Since the display is on the network, *display_name* includes the host name as part of the name. The *display class* can be used to specify resources specific to a particular class of X terminals. (Your X terminal documentation should tell you the display class of your X terminal.) The *display_type* of `foreign` tells the login server to connect to an existing X server rather than to start its own. In this case, an *X_server_command* is not specified.

Controlling Access to the Login Server

By default, any host on your network that has access to your login server host can request a login screen be displayed. You can limit access to the login server by modifying the `Xaccess` file.

To modify `Xaccess`, copy `Xaccess` from `/usr/dt/config` to `/etc/dt/config`. After modifying `/etc/dt/config/Xaccess`, tell the login server to reread `Xaccess` by typing:

```
/usr/dt/bin/dtconfig -reset
```

This issues the command `kill -HUP` *login server process ID*.

XDMCP Direct

When a host attempts to connect to the login server via XDMCP-direct, the host name is compared to the `Xaccess` entries to determine whether the host is allowed access to the login server. Each `Xaccess` entry is a host name including the wildcards `*` (asterisk) and `?` (question mark). An `*` (asterisk) matches zero or more characters and a `?` (question mark) matches any one character. An `!` (exclamation point) prefacing an entry disallows access, while no preface allows access.

For example, if `Xaccess` contains the following three entries:

```
amazon.waterloo.com
*.dept5.waterloo.com
!*
```

The first entry allows access to the login server from host `amazon.waterloo.com`, the second entry allows access from any host whose full domain name ends in `dept5.waterloo.com`, and the last entry disallows access from any other host.

XDMCP Indirect

When a host attempts to connect to the login server via XDMCP-indirect, the host name is compared to the `Xaccess` entries to determine whether the host is allowed access to the login server. Each `Xaccess` entry is similar to the XDMCP-direct entries, including wildcards, except that each entry is marked with a `CHOOSER` string. For example:

```
amazon.waterloo.com    CHOOSER BROADCAST
*.dept5.waterloo.com   CHOOSER BROADCAST
!*      CHOOSER BROADCAST
```

Again, the first entry allows access to the login server from host `amazon.waterloo.com`, the second entry allows access from any host whose full domain name ends in `dept5.waterloo.com`, and the last entry disallows access from any other host.

One of the following can be after the `CHOOSER`:

- `BROADCAST`
- *list of host names*

`BROADCAST` tells the login server to broadcast to the login server sub-network to generate a list of available login server hosts. A list of host names tells the login server to use that list for the list of available login hosts. For example:

```
amazon.waterloo.com    CHOOSER shoal.waterloo.com alum.waterloo.com
*.dept5.waterloo.com   CHOOSER BROADCAST
!*      CHOOSER BROADCAST
```

If `amazon.waterloo.com` connects via XDMCP-indirect, it will be presented a list containing `shoal` and `alum`. If `alice.dept5.waterloo.com` connects, it will be presented with a list of all available login server hosts on the login server sub-network. Other XDMCP-indirect requests will be denied.

An alternative to specifying a list of host names is to define one or more macros containing the list of host names. For example:

```
%list1      shoal.waterloo.com alum.waterloo.com
amazon.waterloo.com   CHOOSER %list1
```

Checking for Errors

By default, the login server logs errors in the `/var/dt/Xerrors` file. To change this, you can set the `Dtlogin.errorLogFile` resource in the `Xconfig` file. The directory specified must exist when the login server is started.

For example, to have the login server log errors in the `/var/mylogs/Dterrors` file, set the following in the `Xconfig` file:

```
Dtlogin.errorLogFile: /var/mylogs/Dterrors
```

When the login server is restarted, the login server will log errors to the `/var/mylogs/Dterrors` file. The `/var/mylogs` directory must exist when the login server is started.

Stopping the Login Server

- To disable login server start up when the system is booted, type:

  ```
  /usr/dt/bin/dtconfig -d
  ```

  This will tell the system not to start the login server when you next reboot.

- To Stop the login server by killing the process ID, type:

  ```
  /usr/dt/bin/dtconfig -kill
  ```

  This issues the command `kill` *login server process ID*)

Note – Killing the login server process terminates all user sessions managed by the login server.

You can also stop the login server by killing the process ID. The login server process ID is stored in `/var/dt/Xpid` or in the file specified in `Xconfig` by the `Dtlogin.pidFile` resource.

If you are logged into the desktop at the time you kill the login server, your desktop session will immediately terminate.

The Login Screen

The login screen displayed by the login server is an attractive alternative to the traditional character-mode login screen and provides capabilities beyond those provided by a character-mode login.

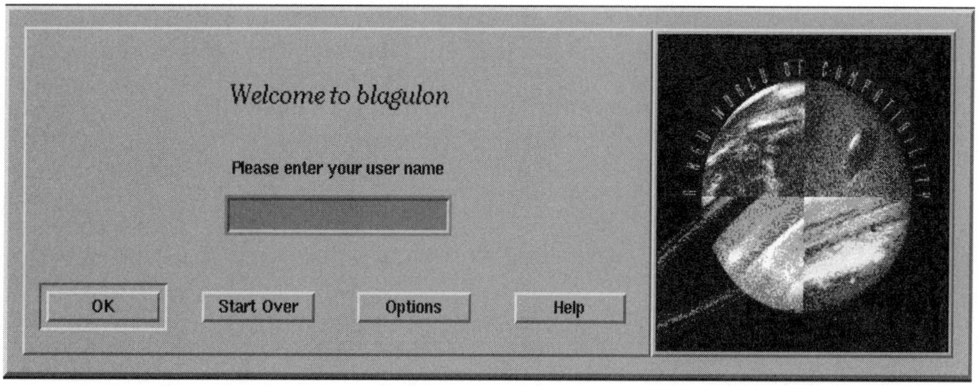

Figure 1-2 Desktop login screen

As with a character mode login, the user enters a user name followed by a password. If authenticated, the login server starts a desktop session for the user. When the user exits the desktop session, the login server displays a new login screen, and the process begins again.

To customize the login screen, you can:

- Change the login screen appearance
- Configure X server authority
- Change the default language
- Issue commands prior to display of the login screen
- Change the contents of the login screen Language menu
- Specify the command to start the user's session
- Issue commands prior to the start of the user's desktop session
- Issue commands after the user's session ends

Each of these can be done for all displays or on a per-display basis.

Changing the Login Screen Appearance

To customize the login screen appearance, you can change the logo or graphic, the welcome messages, and the fonts.

To modify `Xresources`, copy `Xresources` from `/usr/dt/config/`*language* to `/etc/dt/config/`*language*. The login screen will reflect any changes the next time the login screen is displayed. To force a redisplay of a login screen, select Reset Login Screen from the login screen Options menu.

Attributes of the login screen that can be determined by resource specifications in the `Xresources` file include:

`Dtlogin*logo*bitmapFile`	Bitmap or pixmap file to display as logo image
`Dtlogin*greeting*labelString`	Welcome message
`Dtlogin*greeting*persLabelString`	Personalized welcome message
`Dtlogin*greeting*fontList`	Font for welcome messages
`Dtlogin*labelFont`	Font for push buttons and labels
`Dtlogin*textFont`	Font for help and error messages
`Dtlogin*`*language*`*languageName`	Alternate text for locale name *language*

▼ To Change the Logo

♦ Set the `Dtlogin*logo*bitmapFile` resource in `Xresources`.

The logo can be a color pixmap or a bitmap file.

The following example uses the `Mylogo` bitmap as the logo:

```
Dtlogin*logo*bitmapFile: /usr/local/lib/X11/dt/bitmaps/Mylogo.bm
```

▼ To Change the Welcome Message

By default, the login server displays the message `Welcome to` *host name* on the login screen. To change this message:

♦ Set the `Dtlogin*greeting*labelString` resource in `Xresources`.

The value of the `labelString` resource can contain *%LocalHost%*, which will be replaced by the login server host name, and *%DisplayName%*, which will be replaced by the X server display name.

The following example changes the welcome message to `Here's` *host name*`!`:

```
Dtlogin*greeting*labelString: Here's %LocalHost%!
```

Once the user name has been entered, the login server displays the message `Welcome` *username* by default. You can change this message by setting the `Dtlogin*greeting*persLabelString` resource in `Xresources`. The value of the `persLabelString` can contain `%s`, which will be replaced by the *username*.

The following example changes the personalized welcome message to `Hello` *username*.

```
Dtlogin*greeting*persLabelString: Hello %s
```

▼ To Change the Fonts

You can change the fonts used on the login screen by setting one of the following font resources in `Xresources`:

To list the available fonts, type:

`xlsfonts [-`*options*`] [-fn` *pattern*`]`

`Dtlogin*greeting*fontList` Font for welcome messages

`Dtlogin*labelFont` Font for push buttons and labels

`Dtlogin*textFont` Font for help and error messages

The following example uses a large font for the welcome message (the value you specify must be contained on one line):

```
Dtlogin*greeting*fontList: -dt-interface system-medium-r-normal-xxl*-*-*-*-*-*-*-*:
```

To Provide Alternate Text to Display for Each Language

To display per-locale text on the login screen Language menu instead of the default display of the locale name, modify the Dtlogin**language* *languageName resource name resource in Xresources:

```
Dtlogin*En_US*languageName: American
```

The text American will now be displayed rather than the locale name En_US.

Changing the Login Screen Behavior

To customize the login screen behavior, you can modify resources specified in the Xconfig file.

To modify Xconfig, copy Xconfig from /usr/dt/config to /etc/dt/config. After modifying /etc/dt/config/Xconfig, tell the login server to reread Xconfig by typing:

```
/usr/dt/bin/dtconfig -reset
```

This which issues the command kill -HUP *login server process ID*)

Resources specified in the Xconfig file include:

Dtlogin*authorize	Xaccess file specification
Dtlogin*environment	X server environment
Dtlogin*language	Default language
Dtlogin*languageList	Language list for login screen Language menu
Dtlogin*resources	Xresources specification
Dtlogin*setup	Xsetup file specification
Dtlogin*startup	Xstartup file specification
Dtlogin*session	Xsession file specification
Dtlogin*failsafeClient	Xfailsafe script specification
Dtlogin*reset	Xreset script specification
Dtlogin*userPath	PATH for Xsession and Xfailsafe

`Dtlogin*systemPath`	PATH for `Xsetup`, `Xstartup` and `Xfailsafe`
`Dtlogin*systemShell`	SHELL for `Xsetup`, `Xstartup` and `Xfailsafe`
`Dtlogin.timeZone`	TZ for all scripts

Changing the Login Screen Behavior Per Display

In the examples below, changing an `Xconfig` resource changes the login screen behavior for all displays. The resources listed with an * (asterisk) can be specified on a per-display basis. This enables you to specify custom login screen behavior for certain displays. To specify a resource for a particular display, the resource is specified as `Dtlogin*`*displayName*`*`*resource*. For example, if you would like to turn off user based access control for display `expo:0` but leave it on for other displays, you would specify:

```
Dtlogin*expo_0*authorize: False
```

Note – Any special character in the display name, such as a : (colon) or . (period), is replaced by an _ (underbar).

Changing the X Server Access

By default, the login server allows X server access control on a per user basis and is based on authorization data stored and protected in the *HomeDirectory*/`.Xauthority` file. Only users who can read this file are allowed to connect to the X server. Generally, this is the preferred method of X server access control.

An alternative to user-based access control is host-based access control. Using this method, if a host is granted access to the X server, any user on that host is allowed to connect to the X server. Reasons to use host-based control include:

- Older R2 and R3 X clients will not be able to connect to an X server using user-based access control.
- On unsecured networks, a snooper may be able to intercept the authorization data passed between the X client and X server on the network.

The Xconfig Dtlogin*authorize resource tells the login server to use user-based X server access control. To use host-based access control, change the authorize resource value to False, for example:

```
Dtlogin*authorize: False
```

▼ To Change the X Server Environment

If you with to provide the X server with one or more environment variables and values when started by the login server, you can specify them using the Dtlogin*environment resource in Xconfig. For example:

```
Dtlogin*environment: VAR1=foo VAR2=bar
```

will make the variables VAR1 and VAR2 available to the local X server process. These variables will also be exported to the Xsession and Xfailsafe scripts.

▼ To Change the Default Language

When the user logs in to the desktop from the login screen, the user session is run under the locale selected from the Language submenu of the Options menu. If the user does not select a language, the login server default language is used. You can control the value of the default language by setting the Dtlogin*language resource in Xconfig. For example:

```
Dtlogin*language: Ja_JP
```

Check your system documentation to determine the languages installed on your system.

▼ To Change the Content of the Login Screen Language Menu

By default the login server creates the login screen Language menu containing a list of all locales installed on the system. When the user selects a locale from the login screen language list, the login server will redisplay the login screen in the selected locale. When the user subsequently logs in, the login server will start a desktop session for the user in that locale.

You can specify your own list of languages by modifying the Dtlogin*languageList resource in Xconfig:

```
Dtlogin*languageList: En_US De_DE
```

The login server now displays only En_US and De_DE in the login screen Language menu.

Issuing Commands Before the Login Screen Appears

After the X server has started but before the login screen appears, the login server runs the Xsetup script. Xsetup runs with root authority and issues commands needing to be run before the display of the login screen.

To modify Xsetup, copy Xsetup from /usr/dt/config to /etc/dt/config. The next time the login screen is displayed, the modified Xsetup will be run.

Issuing Commands Before Starting the User Session

After the user enters the user name and password and they are authenticated, but before the user session is started, the login server runs the Xstartup script. Xstartup runs with root authority and issues commands needing to be run as root prior to the user session start.

To modify Xstartup, copy Xstartup from /usr/dt/config to /etc/dt/config. The next time the user logs in, the modified Xstartup will be run.

Starting a Desktop Session

By default, the login server starts the user session by running the Xsession script. Xsession runs with the user's authority and issues commands needed to start the desktop.

Note – Do not directly update the Xsession script.

See Chapter 2, "Configuring Session Manager," for information on how to customize the user's desktop session startup.

Starting a Failsafe Session

If the user selects Failsafe Session from the Sessions submenu of the login screen Options menu, the login server runs the `Xfailsafe` script. `Xfailsafe` runs with the user's authority and issues commands needed to start a minimal windowing environment, usually a Terminal window and an optional window manager.

To modify `Xfailsafe`, copy `Xfailsafe` from `/usr/dt/config` to `/etc/dt/config`. The next time the user logs in, the modified `Xfailsafe` will be run.

After the User's Session Ends

After the user exits the desktop or failsafe session, the login server runs the `Xreset` script. `Xreset` runs with root authority and issues commands needing to be run as root after the end of the user's session.

If you wish to modify `Xreset`, copy `Xreset` from `/usr/dt/config` to `/etc/dt/config`. The next time the user logs in, the modified `Xreset` will be run.

The Login Server Environment

The login server provides an environment that it exports to the `Xsetup`, `Xstartup`, `Xsession`, `Xfailsafe` and `Xreset` scripts. This environment is described in Table 1-1. Additional variables may also be exported by the login server.

Table 1-1 Login Server Environments

Environment Variable	`Xsetup`	`Xstartup`	`Xsession`	`Xreset`	Description
LANG	X	X	X	X	Default or selected language
XAUTHORITY	X	X	X	X	Alternate X authority file (optional)
PATH	X	X	X	X	Value of the `Dtlogin*userPath` resource (`Xsession`, `Xfailsafe`) or `Dtlogin*systemPath` resource (`Xsetup`, `Xstartup`, `Xreset`)

Table 1-1 Login Server Environments *(Continued)*

Environment Variable	Xsetup	Xstartup	Xsession	Xreset	Description
DISPLAY	X	X	X	X	X server connection number
SHELL	X	X	X	X	Shell specified in `/etc/passwd` (`Xsession`, `Xfailsafe`) or `Dtlogin*systemShell` resource (`Xsetup`, `Xstartup`, `Xreset`)
TZ	X	X	X	X	Value of `Dtlogin.timeZone` resource or timezone determined from system
USER		X	X	X	User name
HOME		X	X	X	Home directory specified in `/etc/passwd`
LOGNAME		X	X	X	User name

Changing the User or System Path

The login server sets the PATH environment variable when it runs the `Xsession` and `Xfailsafe` scripts. You can provide an alternate path to these scripts

▼ *To Change the User Path*

♦ Set the `Dtlogin*userPath` resource in `Xconfig`. For example:

```
Dtlogin*userPath:/usr/bin:/etc:/usr/sbin:/usr/ucb:/usr/bin/X11
```

▼ *To Change the System Path*

♦ Set the `Dtlogin*systemPath` resource in `Xconfig`. For example:

```
Dtlogin*systemPath: /usr/bin/X11:/etc:/bin:/usr/bin:/usr/ucb
```

▼ To Change the System Shell

The login server sets the SHELL environment variable when it runs the `Xsetup`, `Xstartup` and `Xfailsafe` scripts. The default is `/bin/sh`. If you wish to provide an alternate shell to these scripts, you can set the `Dtlogin*systemShell` resource in `Xconfig`. For example:

```
Dtlogin*systemShell: /bin/ksh
```

▼ To Change the Time Zone

The login server sets the TZ environment variable when it runs the `Xsetup`, `Xstartup`, `Xsession`, `Xfailsafe`, and `Xreset` scripts. The default value is derived from the system so usually you will not need to change this behavior. To provide an alternate time zone to these scripts, set the `Dtlogin.timeZone` resource in `Xconfig`. For example:

```
Dtlogin.timeZone: CST6CDT
```

Administering Login Manager

When the login server starts, one `dtlogin` process is started. The `dtlogin` process reads the `Xconfig` file to determine the initial login server configuration and locate other login server configuration files. The login server then reads the `Xservers` file to see if it has any displays to explicitly manage, and also reads the `Xaccess` file to control access to the login server.

If the login server finds from the `Xservers` file that it needs to manage a local display, it will start an X server as instructed in the `Xservers` file and then display a login screen on that display.

If the login server finds from the `Xservers` file that it needs to manage a network display, it will assume an X server is already running with the specified display name and display a login screen on that display.

The login server will then wait for XDMCP requests from the network.

For each display managed, the login server first creates a new `dtlogin` process for that display. This means if the login server is managing *n* displays, there will be *n+1* `dtlogin` processes. The login server will run the `Xsetup` script, load the `Xresources` file, then run `dtgreet` to display the login screen. Once the user has entered a username and password and has been authenticated, the login server will run the `Xstartup` script and then the `Xsession` or `Xfailsafe` script. When the user has exited the session, the login server will run the `Xreset` script.

If the login server gets an XDMCP-indirect request, it will run `dtchooser` to present a list of login server hosts on the display. When the user selects a host from the list, the login server on that host will manage the display.

For the `Xaccess`, `Xconfig`, `Xfailsafe`, `Xreset`, *language*`/Xresources`, `Xservers`, `Xsetup`, and `Xstartup` configuration files, the login server will by default look first in `/etc/dt/config`, then `/usr/dt/config`, and use the first file found.

Login Manager Files

The default locations of the Login Manager files are:

`/usr/dt/bin/dtlogin`	The login server and display manager
`/usr/dt/bin/dtgreet`	Displays a login screen for a display
`/usr/dt/bin/dtchooser`	Displays a chooser screen for a display
`/usr/dt/bin/Xsession`	Starts a desktop session
`/usr/dt/config/Xfailsafe`	Starts a failsafe session
`/usr/dt/config/Xconfig`	Login server configuration file
`/usr/dt/config/Xservers`	Login server display description file
`/usr/dt/config/Xaccess`	Login server access description file
`/usr/dt/config/`*language*`/Xresources`	Display layout resources
`/usr/dt/config/Xsetup`	Display setup file
`/usr/dt/config/Xstartup`	Pre-session startup file
`/usr/dt/config/Xreset`	Post-session reset file
`/var/dt/Xpid`	Process ID of the login server
`/var/dt/Xerrors`	Error log file of the login server

Configuring Session Manager 2

Session Manager is responsible for starting the desktop and automatically saving and restoring running applications, colors, fonts, mouse behavior, audio volume, and keyboard click.

Using Session Manager, you can:

- Customize the initial session for all desktop users
- Customize the environment and resources for all desktop users
- Change the session startup message
- Change parameters for session startup tools and daemons
- Customize desktop color usage for all users

What Is a Session?

A session is the collection of applications, settings, and resources present on the user's desktop. Session management is a set of conventions and protocols that enables Session Manager to save and restore a user's session. A user is able to log into the system and be presented with the same set of running applications, settings, and resources as were present when the user logged off. When a user logs into the desktop for the first time, a default initial session is loaded. Afterward, Session Manager supports the notion of a current and a home session.

The Initial Session

When a user logs into the desktop for the first time, Session Manager will generate the user's initial session using system default values. By default, the File Manager and Introduction to the Desktop, a help volume, will start.

Current Session

The user's running session is always considered the current session, whether restored upon login from a saved home session, a saved current session, or the system default initial session. Based on the user's Style Manager Startup settings, when the user exits the session, Session Manager automatically saves the current session. When the user next logs in to the desktop, Session Manager restarts the previously saved current session, meaning that the desktop will be restored to same state as when the user last logged out.

Home Session

You can also have the desktop restored to the same state every time the user logs in, regardless of its state when the user logged out. The user can save the state of the current session and then, using the Style Manager Startup settings, have Session Manager start that session every time the user logs in.

Display-Specific Sessions

To run a specific session for a specific display, a user can create a display-specific session. To do this, the user can copy the *HomeDirectory*`/.dt/sessions` directory to *HomeDirectory*`/.dt/`*display*, where *display* is the real, unqualified host name (for example, `pablo:0` is valid, `pablo.gato.com:0` or `unix:0` is not). When the user logs in on display `pablo:0`, Session Manager will start that display-specific session.

DISPLAY = ukaul:0.0

Starting a Session

Session Manager is started through /usr/dt/bin/Xsession. When the user logs in using the Login Manager, Xsession is started by default.

Optionally, the user can log in using the traditional character mode (getty) login, and start Session Manager manually using tools that start an X server, such as xinit. For example: xinit /usr/dt/bin/Xsession.

When a Session Starts

When Session Manager is started, it goes through the following steps to start the user's session:

1. Sources the *HomeDirectory*/.dtprofile script
2. Sources the Xsession.d scripts
3. Displays a welcome message
4. Sets up desktop search paths
5. Gathers available applications
6. Optionally sources *HomeDirectory*/.profile or *HomeDirectory*/.login
7. Starts the ToolTalk® messaging daemon
8. Loads session resources
9. Starts the color server
10. Starts the Workspace Manager
11. Starts the session applications

The following sections describe the steps listed above.

Sourcing the .dtprofile Script

At session startup, the Xsession script sources the user's *HomeDirectory*/.dtprofile script. The *HomeDirectory*/.dtprofile script is a /bin/sh or /bin/ksh script that enables users to set up environment variables for their sessions. For more information on setting up environment variables, see "Additional Session Startup Customizations" on page 32.

If the *HomeDirectory*/.dtprofile script does not exist, such as when a user is logging into the desktop for the first time, Xsession will copy the desktop default sys.dtprofile to *HomeDirectory*/.dtprofile.

The desktop default is /usr/dt/config/sys.dtprofile. To customize the sys.dtprofile script, copy sys.dtprofile from /usr/dt/config to /etc/dt/config and edit the new file.

Sourcing Xsession.d Scripts

After sourcing the *HomeDirectory*/.dtprofile script, the Xsession script sources the Xsession.d scripts. These scripts are used to set up additional environment variables and start optional daemons for the user's session. The default Xsession.d scripts are:

0010.dtpaths	Documents customizable desktop search paths
0020.dtims	Starts optional input method server
0030.dttmpdir	Creates per-user, per-session temporary directory
0040.xmbind	Sets up $XMBINDDIR to desktop default

There may be additional vendor-specific scripts in Xsession.d.

Xsession first sources all files in the /etc/dt/config/Xsession.d directory, followed by those in the /usr/dt/config/Xsession.d directory.

The desktop default Xsession.d scripts are located in the /usr/dt/config/Xsession.d directory. To customize an Xsession.d script, copy the script from /usr/dt/config/Xsession.d to /etc/dt/config/Xsession.d and edit the new file. You must have execute permission to perform this task.

Also, to have Xsession automatically source a script of your own, copy it to /etc/dt/config/Xsession.d.

Note – When you modify or create an Xsession.d script, make sure that any foreground commands you issue are of short duration, as the time taken by the command will directly affect session startup time. If a foreground command does not exit, the session startup will hang. Commands run in an Xsession.d script that you want to remain running for the duration of the session should be run in the background.

Displaying the Welcome Message

After sourcing *HomeDirectory*/.dtprofile and the Xsession.d scripts, Xsession displays a welcome message that covers the screen. You can customize the welcome message displayed, or turn off the message entirely. The dthello client is used to display the message.

To alter the message text, change the dthello options by modifying the dtstart_hello[0] variable.

To change dtstart_hello[0], create an /etc/dt/config/Xsession.d script that sets the new value. To display the message of the day for all users, create an executable sh or ksh script, for example /etc/dt/config/Xsession.d/*myvars*, and set dtstart_hello[0] as follows:

```
dtstart_hello[0]="/usr/dt/bin/dthello -file /etc/motd &"
```

Similarly, users can change the welcome message for their sessions by setting dtstart_hello[0] in *HomeDirectory*/.dtprofile.

To turn off the welcome message, set dtstart_hello[0]=" ".

For more information about dthello, see the dthello man page.

Setting Up the Desktop Search Paths

The desktop search paths are created at login by dtsearchpath. There are two categories of environment variables used by dtsearchpath:

Input Variables	System-wide and personal environment variables whose values are set by the system administrator or end user.
Output Variables	Variables created and assigned values by dtsearchpath. The value of each variable is the search path for the desktop session.

To alter the command-line options of dtsearchpath, modify the dtstart_searchpath variable. To change the dtstart_searchpath variable for all users, create an executable sh or ksh script (for example /etc/dt/config/Xsession.d/*myvars*), and set dtstart_searchpath as follows:

```
dtstart_searchpath="/usr/dt/bin/dtsearchpath"
```

Users can similarly change the `dtsearchpath` options for their own sessions only by setting `dtstart_searchpath` in *HomeDirectory*`/.dtprofile`.

For more information about `dtsearchpath`, see Chapter 7, "Desktop Search Paths." For more information about `dtsearchpath` options, see the `dtsearchpath` man page.

Gathering Available Applications

The next step after setting up the desktop search paths is to gather available applications, using `dtappgather`. To alter the command-line options of `dtappgather`, modify the `dtstart_appgather` variable. To change the `dtstart_appgather` variable for all users, create an executable `sh` or `ksh` script (for example `/etc/dt/config/Xsession.d/`*myvars*), and set `dtstart_appgather` as follows:

```
dtstart_appgather="/usr/dt/bin/dtappgather &"
```

Users can similarly change the `dtappgather` options for their own sessions only by setting `dtstart_appgather` in *HomeDirectory*`/.dtprofile`.

For more information about `dtappgather` options, see the `dtappgather (4)` man page.

Optionally Sourcing the .profile or .login Script

`Xsession` is able to source a user's traditional *HomeDirectory*`/.profile` or *HomeDirectory*`/.login` scripts. By default this capability is disabled. To tell `Xsession` to source the `.profile` or `.login` script, set `DTSOURCEPROFILE` to `true`.

To change `DTSOURCEPROFILE` for all users, create an `/etc/dt/config/Xsession.d` script that sets the new value. To set `DTSOURCEPROFILE` to `true` for all users, create an executable `sh` or `ksh` script, for example `/etc/dt/config/Xsession.d/`*myvars*, and set `DTSOURCEPROFILE` as follows:

```
DTSOURCEPROFILE=true
```

Users can similarly change `DTSOURCEPROFILE` for their own sessions by setting `DTSOURCEPROFILE` to `true` in *HomeDirectory*`/.dtprofile`.

Starting the ToolTalk Messaging Daemon

The ToolTalk messaging daemon, `ttsession`, enables independent applications to communicate with each other without having direct knowledge of each other. Applications create and send ToolTalk messages to communicate with each other. `ttsession` communicates on the network to deliver messages.

To alter the command-line options of `ttsession`, modify the `dtstart_ttsession` variable. To change the `dtstart_ttsession` variable for all users, create an executable `sh` or `ksh` script (for example `/etc/dt/config/Xsession.d/`*myvars*), and set `dtstart_ttsession` as follows:

```
dtstart_ttsession="/usr/dt/bin/ttsession -s"
```

Users can similarly change the `ttsession` options for their own sessions by setting `dtstart_ttsession` in *HomeDirectory*`/.dtprofile`.

For more information about `ttsession` options, see the `ttsession` man page. For more information on `ttsession`, see *Getting Started Using ToolTalk Messaging*.

Starting the Session Manager Client

At this point, `Xsession` starts `/usr/dt/bin/dtsession`, which continues the session startup process.

Loading the Session Resources

Session Manager uses the X server `RESOURCE_MANAGER` property to make desktop resources available to all applications. Session Manager loads the `RESOURCE_MANAGER` by:

- Loading the system default resources
- Merging any system-wide resources specified by the system administrator.
- Merging any user-specified resources

The desktop default resources can be found in `/usr/dt/config/`*language*`/sys.resources`. These resources will be made available to each user's session via the `RESOURCE_MANAGER` property. This file should not be edited, as it is overwritten upon subsequent desktop installations.

You can augment the system default resources by creating `/etc/dt/config/`*language*`/sys.resources`. In this file, you can override default resources or specify additional resources for all desktop users. Since this file is merged into the desktop default resources during session startup, only new or updated resource specifications should be placed in this file. Resources specified in this file will be made available to each user's session through the `RESOURCE_MANAGER` property. Resources specified in this file take precedence over those specified in the desktop default resource file.

Users can augment the desktop default and system-wide resources using their *HomeDirectory*`/.Xdefaults` file. Resources specified in this file will be made available to that user's session through the `RESOURCE_MANAGER` property. Resources specified in this file take precedence over those specified in the desktop default or system administrator resource files.

Note – The X Toolkit Intrinsics utility specifies that it will load resources for an application from either `RESOURCE_MANAGER` or from *HomeDirectory*`/.Xdefaults`, but not both. Ordinarily, this would mean that the user's *HomeDirectory*`/.Xdefaults` file would be ignored. However, Session Manager accommodates *HomeDirectory*`/.Xdefaults` by merging it into the `RESOURCE_MANAGER` at session startup as described above. If a user changes *HomeDirectory*`/.Xdefaults`, the changes will not be visible to new applications until the user invokes the Reload Resources action. The Reload Resources action will instruct Session Manager to reload the `RESOURCE_MANAGER` with the default, system-wide, and user-specified resources. This makes changes to the system-wide and personal resource files available to applications.

For more information see:

- "Setting Application Resources" on page 256
- The `dtresourcesfile(4)` man page

Starting the Color Server

Session Manager serves as the color server for the desktop and provides the following set of `dtsession` resources that can be used to configure it.

`foregroundColor`	Controls whether a pixel is allocated for the foreground color

`dynamicColor`	Specifies whether read-only colors are allocated
`shadowPixmaps`	Specifies whether colors are allocated for top shadow or bottom shadow
`colorUse`	Limits color allocation
`writeXrdbColors`	Specifies whether the `*background` and `*foreground` resources are placed in the resource database

You can set color server resources for all users by creating `/etc/dt/config/`*language*`/sys.resources` and specifying the color server resources in that file.

Users can similarly set color server resources for their own sessions by specifying color server resources in *HomeDirectory*`/.Xdefaults`.

For more information about setting color server resources, see "Administering Colors" on page 265.

Starting Workspace Manager

Session Manager is responsible for starting Workspace Manager. By default `/usr/dt/bin/dtwm` is started. An alternate window manager can be specified with the `wmStartupCommand` resource.

You can specify an alternate window manager for all users by creating `/etc/dt/config/`*language*`/sys.resources` and specifying the full path name and options for the window manager with the `Dtsession*wmStartupCommand` resource in that file.

Users can similarly specify an alternate window manager for their own sessions only by specifying the `Dtsession*wmStartupCommand` resource in *HomeDirectory*`/.Xdefaults`.

For more information about the Window Manager, see Chapter 14, "Customizing the Workspace Manager."

Starting the Session Applications

At session startup, Session Manager will restart any applications that were saved as part of the session. The system default set of applications to be restored as part of the user's initial session can be found in `/usr/dt/config/`*language*`/sys.session`. This file should not be edited as it will be unconditionally overwritten upon subsequent desktop installations.

For more information, see the `dtsessionfile(4)` man page.

A system administrator can replace the set of applications that are started as part of the user's initial session by copying `/usr/dt/config/`*language*`/sys.session` to `/etc/dt/config/`*language*`/sys.session` and modifying the latter file. Unlike the resource files, this file will be used as a complete replacement for the desktop default file, so you can make a copy of the system default file and make any necessary modifications.

Additional Session Startup Customizations

This section covers:

- Setting environment variables
- Setting resources
- Using display-dependent sessions
- Running scripts at login
- Recovering a back-up session

▼ To Set Environment Variables

♦ To set system-wide environment variables, create a file in the `/etc/dt/config/Xsession.d` directory that sets and exports the variable.

For example, if you create an executable `ksh` script, `/etc/dt/config/Xsession.d/`*myvars*,

containing:

```
export MYVARIABLE="value"
```

then the variable `MYVARIABLE` will be set in each user's environment at the next login.

♦ To set personal environment variables, set the variable in *HomeDirectory*/`.dtprofile`.

For example:

```
export MYVARIABLE="value"
```

sets the variable `MYVARIABLE` in each user's environment at the next login.

Note – Session Manager does not automatically read the `.profile` or `.login` file. However, it can be configured to use these files; see "Optionally Sourcing the .profile or .login Script" on page 28.

▼ To Set Resources

♦ To set system-wide resources, add the resources to the file `/etc/dt/config/`*language*`/sys.resources`. (You may have to create the file.)

Note – `.dtprofile` only supports `/bin/sh` or `/bin/ksh` syntax.

For example, if in `/etc/dt/config/C/sys.resources` you specify:

```
AnApplication*resource: value
```

then the resource `AnApplication*resource` will be set in each user's `RESOURCE_MANAGER` property at the next login.

♦ To set personal resources, add the resources to the file *HomeDirectory*/`.Xdefaults`.

▼ To Set Display-Specific Resources

You can set display-specific resources for all desktop users on the system. Also, users can set display-specific resources limited to their own session. This enables you to specify resources depending upon which display the user uses to log in to the desktop.

♦ To set display-specific resources for all desktop users on the system, create the file `/etc/dt/config/`*language*`/sys.resources` that specifies the display-specific resources.

- To set personal display-specific resources, specify the resource in *HomeDirectory*/.Xdefaults.

You delimit these resources by enclosing them in cpp conditional statements. A DISPLAY_*displayname* macro is defined depending upon the value of the $DISPLAY variable. This is done by converting all . (period) and : (colon) characters to _ (underscores), stripping off any screen specification, and finally prefixing DISPLAY_ to the result.

For example, a $DISPLAY of :0 would be DISPLAY_0, and a $DISPLAY of blanco.gato.com:0.0 would be DISPLAY_blanco_gato_com_0. The resulting value can be used as part of a cpp test in a session resource file. For example, if in /etc/dt/config/C/sys.resources you specify:

```
Myapp*resource: value

#ifdef DISPLAY_blanco_gato_com_0
Myapp*resource: specialvalue1
#endif

#ifdef DISPLAY_pablo_gato_com_0
Myapp*resource: specialvalue2
#endif
```

the resource MyApp*resource will be set in RESOURCE_MANAGER to specialvalue1 when the user logs in on display blanco.gato.com:0; specialvalue2 when the user logs in on pablo.gato.com:0; and value when the user logs in on another display.

▼ To Change Applications for the Initial Session

You can specify alternate applications to start as part of a user's initial session.

1. Copy /usr/dt/config/*language*/sys.session to /etc/dt/config/*language*/sys.session.
2. Modify the new sys.session file.

   Each entry in sys.session appears as:

   ```
   dtsmcmd -cmd command_and_options
   ```

   To start an additional application as part of a user's initial session, specify a new sys.session entry with a full path name. For example, to start /usr/bin/X11/xclock as part of a user's initial session, add an xclock entry to /etc/dt/config/C/sys.session:

```
#
# Start up xclock...
#
dtsmcmd -cmd "/usr/bin/X11/xclock -digital"
```

▼ To Set Up a Display-Specific Session

A user can set up a display-specific session to tune a session to a particular display.

♦ Copy the *HomeDirectory*/`.dt/sessions` directory to *HomeDirectory*/`.dt/`*display* where *display* is the real, unqualified host name (`pablo:0` is valid, `pablo.gato.com:0` or `unix:0` is not).

For example, to create a display-specific session for display `pablo.gato.com:0`:

`cp -r` *HomeDirectory*/`.dt/sessions` *HomeDirectory*/`.dt/pablo:0`

When the user next logs in on display `pablo.gato.com:0`, the Session Manager will start that display-specific session.

Executing Additional Commands at Session Startup and Logout

Users can specify that additional commands be started when they log in to their desktop sessions. This is useful for setting up X settings that are not saved by Session Manager. For example, the user can use `xsetroot` to customize the root (workspace) pointer. Another use would be to start applications that are unable to be saved and restored by Session Manager. If an application will not restart when the session is restored, the user can start the client using this method.

▼ To Execute Additional Commands at Session Startup

♦ Create the file *HomeDirectory*/`.dt/sessionetc` containing the commands.

Generally this file is a script and must have execute permission. Processes started in `sessionetc` should be run in the background.

Note – Do not use `sessionetc` to start clients that are automatically restored by Session Manager. Doing so can cause multiple copies of the application to be started. You may not be able to see the copies immediately because the windows may be stacked on top of one another.

▼ To Execute Additional Commands at Logout

A companion file to `sessionetc` is `sessionexit`. Use `sessionexit` to perform some operation at session exit that is not handled by Session Manager.

♦ Create the file *HomeDirectory*`/.dt/sessionexit`.

Like `sessionetc`, this file is usually a script with execute permission.

▼ To Recover a Session from Backup

When Session Manager saves a session, the session information is stored in the *HomeDirectory*`/.dt/sessions` directory or in the *HomeDirectory*`/.dt/`*display* directory if using a display-specific session. In these directories, Session Manager creates a subdirectory named `current` or `home` to store information for the respective current or home session. Before the session information is stored, Session Manager makes a backup of the prior session with that name and stores it in `current.old` or `home.old`.

1. Log in using the Failsafe Session or Command Line Login from the login screen.
2. Copy the backup session directory to the active name. For example, to recover the backup home session:

```
cp -r HomeDirectory/.dt/sessions/home.old HomeDirectory/.dt/sessions/home
```

Display-specific sessions can be recovered in the same manner.

▼ To Investigate Session Startup Problems

♦ Check the file *HomeDirectory*/.dt/startlog.

Session Manager logs each user's session startup progress in this file.

Session Manager Files and Directories

- /usr/dt/bin/Xsession
- /usr/dt/config/Xsession.d/*
- /usr/dt/bin/dtsession
- /usr/dt/bin/dtsession_res
- *HomeDirectory*/.dt/sessions/current
- *HomeDirectory*/.dt/sessions/home
- *HomeDirectory*/.dt/*display*/current
- *HomeDirectory*/.dt/*display*/home

Adding and Administering Applications

3

Application Manager is the desktop container for applications available to the user.

Structure of Application Manager

The top level of Application Manager generally contains directories. Each of these directories, and its contents, is called an *application group*.

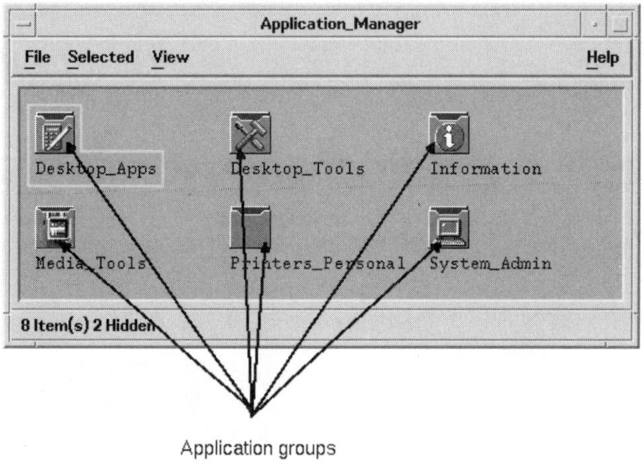

Figure 3-1 Application groups in Application Manager

The application groups and their contents are gathered from multiple locations locally and throughout the network.

Directory Location of Application Manager

In the file system, Application Manager is the directory `/var/dt/appconfig/appmanager/`*login-hostname-display*. The directory is created dynamically each time the user logs in.

For example, if user `ronv` logs in from display `wxyz:0`, the Application Manager directory `/var/dt/appconfig/appmanager/ronv-wxyz-0` is created.

How Application Manager Finds and Gathers Applications

Application Manager is built by gathering local and remote application groups. The application groups are gathered from directories located along the application search path.

The default application search path consists of these locatio

Scope	Location
Built-in	/usr/dt/appconfig/appmanager/*language*
System-wide	/etc/dt/appconfig/appmanager/*language*
Personal	*HomeDirectory*/.dt/appmanager

To create the top level of Application Manager, links are created at login time from the application groups (directories) located in directories on the application search path to the Application Manager directory /var/dt/appconfig/appmanager/*login-hostname-display*. The gathering operation is done by the desktop utility dtappgather, which is automatically run by Login Manager after the user has successfully logged in.

For example, the desktop provides the built-in application group:

/usr/dt/appconfig/appmanager/*language*/Desktop_Tools

At login time, a symbolic link is created to:

/var/dt/appconfig/appmanager/*login-hostname-display*/Desktop_Tools

The application search path can include remote directories. This provides a way to gather application groups from systems located throughout the network. For more information, see "Adding an Application Server to the Application Search Path" on page 47.

Precedence Rules in Gathering Applications

Where duplicates exist along the search path, personal application groups have precedence over system-wide groups, and system-wide groups have precedence over built-in groups. For example, if both /usr/dt/appconfig/appmanager/C/Desktop_Tools and /etc/dt/appconfig/appmanager/C/Desktop_Tools exist, the application group under /etc will be the one used.

Application Groups Provided with the Default Desktop

The uncustomized desktop provides four application groups.

- Desktop_Apps
- Desktop_Tools

- Information
- System_Admin

Example of How Application Groups Are Gathered

Figure 3-2 shows an Application Manager window containing a variety of application groups. Table 3-1 shows the directories from which the application groups were gathered.

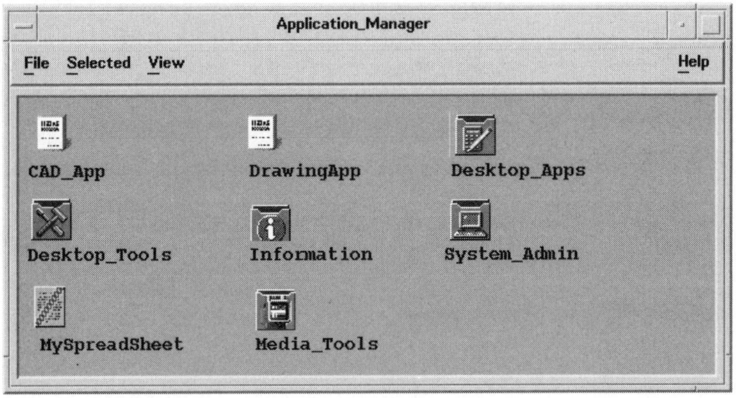

Figure 3-2 A typical Application Manager window

Table 3-1 Source of Application Groups for Figure 3-2

Name	Directory Gathered
CAD_App	`/net/ApServA/etc/dt/appconfig/appmanager/C/CAD_App`
DrawingApp	`/etc/dt/appconfig/appmanager/C/DrawingApp`
Desktop_Apps	`/usr/dt/appconfig/appmanager/C/Desktop_Apps`
Desktop_Tools	`/usr/dt/appconfig/appmanager/C/Desktop_Tools`
Information	`/usr/dt/appconfig/appmanager/C/Information`
System_Admin	`/etc/dt/appconfig/appmanager/C/System_Admin`
MySpreadSheet	`/users/anna/.dt/appmanager/MySpreadSheet`
Media_Tools	`/etc/dt/appconfig/appmanager/C/Media_Tools`

If the Information or System_Admin application groups have been customized, they will be gathered from `/etc/dt/appconfig/appmanager/C` instead.

The CAD_App group is gathered because a system named `ApServA` has been added to the application search path (see "Adding an Application Server to the Application Search Path" on page 47). MySpreadSheet is a personal application group, available only to user `anna`.

Adding Applications to Application Manager

When an application has been added to Application Manager, there is an icon in an application group that starts that application.

Many applications provide an application group. The application group is a directory at the top level of Application Manager that contains the application icon and other files related to the application.

Some applications may not have their own application group. Instead, the icon to start the application is located in a general application group. For example, you could create an empty application group named "Games" that you use as a container for all the games you install on the system.

Ways to Add Applications to Application Manager

There are two ways to add an application to Application Manager:

- Registering the application
- Adding an application icon without registering the application

Registering the Application

Application registration provides full application integration.

A registered application:

- Has its own application group.
- Has its desktop configuration files gathered under a single location. This group of desktop configuration files is called the *registration package*.
- May have a registered help volume.

There are two ways an application can become registered:

- When you install a desktop-smart application, registration occurs automatically. See "To Add a Desktop-Smart Application to Application Manager" on page 44.

- An existing application can be registered by creating a registration package. See "To Register an Existing or Non-Desktop Smart Application" on page 45.

The use of a registration package makes the application easier to administer on the desktop. The registration package is created somewhere in the file system other than the locations used for desktop configuration files.

Adding the Application without Using a Registration Package.

This is the preferred way to add application when you want Application Manager to contain only an icon to start the application.

An application added without using a registration package:

- May have its own application group, but usually has its icon placed in an existing application group
- Has its desktop configuration files placed directly in locations along the desktop's search paths.

See "To Add an Application Icon to an Existing Application Group" on page 45.

▼ To Add a Desktop-Smart Application to Application Manager

A desktop-smart application is an application that is automatically registered into Application Manager when the application is installed. The application's filesets include the registration package required by the desktop.

1. Install the application using instructions provided with the application.
2. When installation is complete, double-click Reload Applications in the Desktop_Tools application group.
3. Verify that installation is complete:
   a. Open Application Manager and check for the presence of the new application group.
   b. To open the application, open the application group and double-click the application's icon.

▼ To Register an Existing or Non-Desktop Smart Application

This is the preferred way to fully integrate an application into the desktop.

The desktop provides a tool, `dtappintegrate`, that creates links between the registration package files and the directories on the desktop search path.

Desktop registration is explained in Chapter 4, "Registering an Application."

▼ To Add an Application Icon to an Existing Application Group

This procedure explains how to add an application icon to an existing application group.

For example, the desktop provides an application group named System_Admin that has been reserved for various applications and scripts related to administering systems. If you have a script that users frequently run, you might want users to be able to run the script by double-clicking an icon in the System_Admin application group.

1. Use Create Action to create an action definition for the application.

   For more information about Create Action, see Chapter 9, "Creating Actions and Data Types Using Create Action."

2. Create an executable file with the same name as the action name in the directory for the application group. The content of the file is irrelevant.

   For example, if you've created an action named "Cleanup" that runs a system administration tool, you would create the executable file `/etc/dt/appconfig/appmanager/`*language*`/System_Admin/Cleanup`.

Creating and Administering General Application Groups

A general application is an application group (directory) that is not associated with one particular application product. For example, the built-in Desktop_Tools application group is a general group containing icons for a large number of applications that a related, but not part of a single product.

You can create additional general application groups. For example, you might want to create a group called Games to group together the various games available on the system.

A general application group can be system-wide or personal in scope.

▼ To Create a System-Wide General Application Group

1. Log in as root.
2. Create a directory in `/etc/dt/appconfig/appmanager/`*language*.

   The name of the directory becomes the name of the application group.
3. Double-click Reload Applications in the Desktop_Tools application group.

▼ To Create a Personal General Application Group

1. Create a directory in *HomeDirectory*`/.dt/appmanager`.

   The name of the directory becomes the name of the application group.
2. Double-click Reload Applications in the Desktop_Tools application group.

▼ To Customize a Built-In Application Group

1. Log in as root.
2. If the application group is located in `/usr/dt/appconfig/appmanager/`*language*, copy the application group to `/etc/dt/appconfig/appmanager/`*language*.

   For example, the following command copies the Desktop_Tools application group:

```
cp -r /usr/dt/appconfig/appmanager/C/Desktop_Tools /etc/dt/appconfig/appmanager/C
```

   The new copy of the application group will have precedence over the built-in version.
3. Modify the copy of the application group. For example, you can add new action files (executable files with the same name as actions).
4. To see the changes, log out and back in.

Modifying the Search Path Used To Locate Applications

The major reason for modifying the application search path is to add an application server. When you add an application server to the search path, Application Manager gathers all the server's system-wide application groups.

For more information on the application search path, see "Application Search Path" on page 116.

The Default Search Path

The default application search path includes these directories:

Scope	**Search Path Directory**
Personal	*HomeDirectory*/`.dt/appmanager`
System-wide	`/etc/dt/appconfig/appmanager/`*language*
Built-in	`/usr/dt/appconfig/appmanager/`*language*

Adding an Application Server to the Application Search Path

In addition to modifying the application search path, it may be necessary to perform additional configuration tasks to enable communication with the application server. See "Administering Application Services" on page 99.

▼ *To Set a System-Wide Application Search Path*

1. Log in as root.
2. If the file `/etc/dt/config/Xsession.d/0010.dtpaths` doesn't exist, create it by copying `/usr/dt/config/Xsession.d/0010.dtpaths`.
3. Open `/etc/dt/Xsession.d/0010.paths` for editing. Add or edit a line that sets and exports the `DTSPSYSAPPHOSTS` variable:

   `export DTSPSYSAPPHOSTS=`*hostname*`:[,hostname]`

   For example, the following line adds the system `ApServA` to the application search path:

   ```
   export DTSPSYSAPPHOSTS=ApServA:
   ```

4. Inform all users on the system that they must log out and then log back in for the change to take effect.

▼ To Set a Personal Application Search Path

1. Open *HomeDirectory*/.dtprofile for editing.
2. Add or edit a line that sets and exports the DTSPUSERAPPHOSTS variable:

   ```
   export DTSPUSERAPPHOSTS=hostname:[,hostname]
   ```

   For example, the following line adds the systems ApServB and ApServC to the application search path:

   ```
   export DTSPUSERAPPHOSTS=ApServB:,ApServC:
   ```

3. Log out and then log back in.

General Application Manager Administration

General Application Manager administration tasks include:

- Removing an application
- Rereading the database of applications during a session

▼ To Remove an Application

If an application has been registered using the dtappintegrate tool, you can also use dtappintegrate to reverse the process. When an application is unregistered, its application group is removed from Application Manager, and its actions, data types, icons, and help are no longer available.

1. Log in as root.
2. Run the command:

   ```
   dtappintegrate -s app_root -u
   ```

▼ To Update Application Manager During a Session

You must rebuild Application Manager if you add applications and want those changes to take effect immediately.

♦ Open the Desktop_Tools application group and double-click Reload Applications.

Reload Applications is useful for updating Application Manager when applications are added to an application server. However, Reload Applications does not detect applications that have been removed from an application server, or applications that have been moved from one location to another. These changes take effect when the user logs out and back in.

Changing the Text Editor and Terminal Emulator

Both the text editor and terminal emulator applications can be started by choosing a control in the Front Panel, or by double-clicking an icon in Application Manager.

These applications are also started by other desktop activities.

- The text editor application opens when the user selects a text file in File Manager and chooses Open from the Selected menu. The default text editor is `dtpad`.
- A terminal emulator runs when a user chooses Open Terminal from File Manager's File menu, or when an action opens a terminal emulator window. The default terminal emulator is `dtterm`.

You can configure the desktop to use a different text editor or terminal emulator application in these situations.

▼ To Change the Default Text Editor or Terminal Emulator

1. If the change is system-wide, log in as root.
2. Create an action for the new text editor or terminal emulator application.

- You can use the Create Action application. Figure 3-3 shows a Create Action window filled in for an application named TextPad. For more information about Create Action, see Chapter 9, "Creating Actions and Data Types Using Create Action."

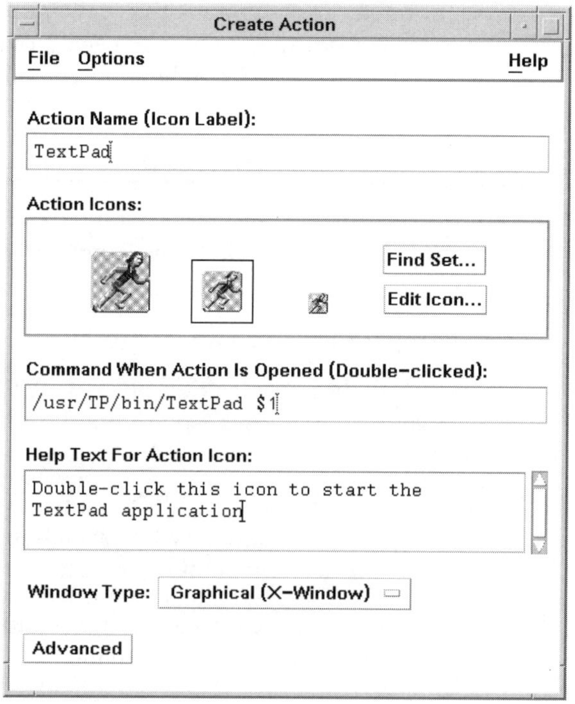

Figure 3-3 Create Action window

- *Or,* you can create the action definition manually; for example:.

```
ACTION TextPad
{
   LABEL           TextPad
   TYPE            COMMAND
   WINDOW_TYPE     NO_STDIO
   EXEC_STRING     /usr/TP/bin/TextPad %(File)Arg_1%
   DESCRIPTION     Double-click this icon to start the \
                   TextPad application.
}
```

For information on creating action definitions manually, see Chapter 10, "Creating Actions Manually."

3. Place the configuration file containing the new action in the proper directory:
   - System-wide: /etc/dt/appconfig/types/*language*
   - Personal: *HomeDirectory*/.dt/types
4. If it doesn't already exist, create the appropriate user-prefs.dt file by copying /usr/dt/appconfig/types/*language*/user-prefs.dt to:
   - System-wide: the /etc/dt/appconfig/types/*language* directory
   - Personal: the *HomeDirectory*/.dt/types directory
5. Edit the TextEditor or Terminal action in the system-wide or personal user-prefs.dt file. Modify the MAP_ACTION line to map the action to the new action.

   For example, change the line:

   ```
   MAP_ACTION Dtpad
   ```

   to:

   ```
   MAP_ACTION TxtPd
   ```
6. Save the user-prefs.dt file.
7. Double-click Reload Actions in the Desktop_Tools application group to reload the actions database.

Registering an Application 4

This chapter describes how to create a registration package for an application and how to register the application onto the desktop.

When an application is fully registered onto the desktop, it has:

- Its own application group at the top level of the Application Manager
- An action that starts the application. The action is represented by an icon in the application group
- Optionally, data types for its data files

Application registration is a non-invasive operation to the application:

- It does not involve modification of the application executable itself. Therefore, you can register existing applications on a system.
- It does not require that any of the application's delivered files (such as the executable and `app-defaults`) be moved to other file locations.
- It can be undone easily. The `dtappintegrate` tool, which is used to register applications, provides a command-line option for reversing the process.

You will want to create a registration package if you are:

- A system administrator who wants to register an existing application onto the desktop
- A software programmer who wants to create an installation package for a desktop-smart application

Overview of Application Registration

This section explains:

- The purpose of application registration
- Features provided to your application by application registration

---

Note – For a detailed example that shows how to register an existing application, see "Example of Creating a Registration Package" on page 77.

Features Provided by Application Registration

Application registration provides a graphical way for users to:

- Locate your application.

Upon installation, your application is “registered” into the Application Manager and has its own application group.

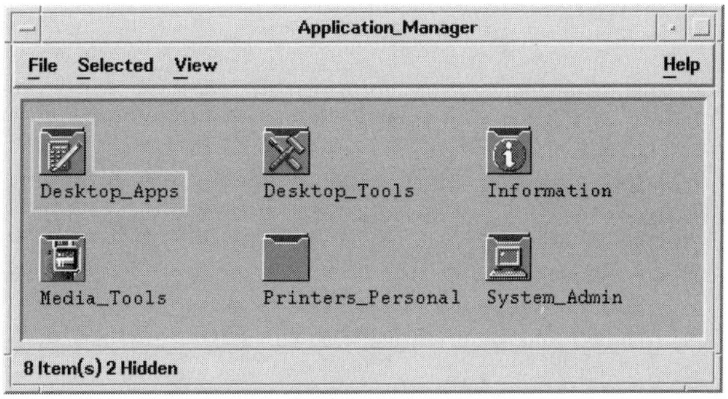

Figure 4-1 Application groups at the top level of Application Manager

- Start your application.

  The application group for your application contains an icon the user can double-click to start your application.

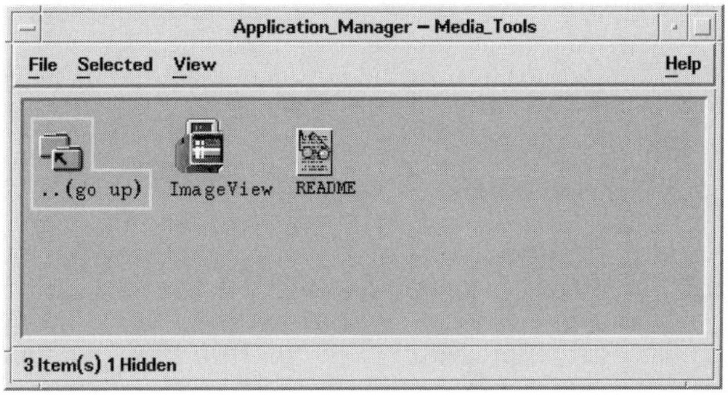

Figure 4-2 An application group containing an icon to start the application

- Identify and manipulate data files. The application's data files will have a unique icon in File Manager.

The user can use data file icons to:

- Start (Open) the application
- Print data files

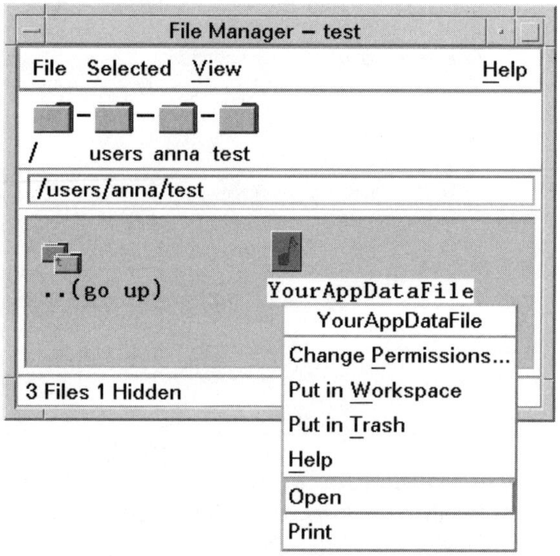

Figure 4-3 A data file's pop-up menu containing "Open" and "Print"

- Perform other operations, such as mailing, compressing, viewing, or playing (audio) data

The Purpose of Application Registration

A registered desktop application has certain configuration files used by the desktop to provide the application's user interface:

- Action and data type definition files
- Icon image (pixmap or bitmap) files
- A directory and files that create the application group
- Optionally, desktop help files and Front Panel definition files

In order for these files to be recognized and used by the desktop, they must be in certain directories specified by the desktop's search paths.

It can be difficult to administer an application when its configuration files are scattered among numerous directories. Therefore, the desktop allows an application to keep all its desktop configuration files gathered under a single directory. This grouping of files is called a *registration package.*

If the application is desktop smart, it supplies a registration package as part of its installation package. If you are a system administrator creating the configuration files yourself, you can create the registration package yourself.

The configuration files in the registration package are not available to the desktop because they are not located in the proper search path directories. The process of placing these files in the proper locations is called *registering*, or *integrating*, the application.

The desktop provides a tool, `dtappintegrate`, that performs the registration by creating symbolically linked representations of the files in the proper search path directories.

Many desktop-smart applications will automatically run `dtappintegrate` during the installation process. If you are a system administrator integrating an existing application, you can run it yourself after you've created the registration package.

Once an application is registered on a system's desktop, the application is available to all users on the system. If the system is configured as a desktop application server, the application will also be available to other systems throughout the network.

The `dtappintegrate` tool has a command-line option that reverses the process by breaking the links. This makes it easy to remove the application from the Application Manager so that it can be moved to a different application server or updated.

General Steps for Registering an Application

Note – For a detailed example that uses these steps to create an application package, see "Example of Creating a Registration Package" on page 77.

---

1. Modify any application resources that set fonts and colors. Otherwise, the desktop's dynamic fonts and colors will not work properly.

   See "Step 1: Modifying Font and Color Resources" on page 58.

2. Create an application root location.

   See "Step 2: Creating the Desktop Application Root" on page 60.

3. Create the directory structure underneath the application root.

   See "Step 3: Creating the Registration Package Directories" on page 60

4. Create the actions and data types for the application.

   See "Step 4: Creating the Actions and Data Types for the Application" on page 62.

5. Put the help files in an appropriate directory.

   See "Step 5: Putting the Help Files in the Registration Package" on page 66.

6. Create the icons for the application

   See "Step 6: Creating Icons for the Application" on page 67.

7. Create the application group for the application.

   See "Step 7: Creating the Application Group" on page 68.

8. Register the application using `dtappintegrate`.

   See "Step 8: Registering the Application Using dtappintegrate" on page 75.

Step 1: Modifying Font and Color Resources

Note – For an example of modifying resources for an application, see Step 1 of the "Example of Creating a Registration Package" on page 78.

The desktop provides mechanisms for setting and manipulating interface fonts and window colors. In order for an application to use these mechanisms properly, you may have to modify the application's `app-defaults` file.

Modifying Font Resources

Note – This section applies to applications created using OSF/Motif 1.2™ (or later versions). Style Manager cannot set interface fonts for applications written using earlier versions of OSF/Motif.

The desktop Style Manager will set interface fonts for applications created using OSF/Motif 1.2 (or later versions) if the application does not specify application-specific interface fonts.

Style Manager provides two fonts:

system font	Used by system areas such as labels, menus, and buttons
user font	Used for editable areas such as text fields

Each font is provided in seven sizes, labeled 1 through 7 in the Fonts dialog box. The Style Manager fonts are connected to actual fonts on the system through Style Manager resources set in `/usr/dt/app-defaults/`*language*`/Dtstyle`.

If you want the application to use the Style Manager fonts, you should remove any application resources that interface specify fonts. The desktop will automatically set the application's resources appropriately:

`FontList`	Set to system font
`XmText*FontList`	Set to user font
`XmTextField*FontList`	Set to user font

Modifying Color Resources

Style Manager provides the ability to change application colors dynamically. The application must be an OSF/Motif 1.1 or 1.2 client. Clients written with other toolkits cannot change color dynamically; color changes take effect when the client is restarted.

The easiest way to use the dynamic colors provided by the desktop is to remove any application color resources for background and foreground color.

Step 2: Creating the Desktop Application Root

Note – For an example of creating the desktop application root directory for an application, see Step 2 of "Example of Creating a Registration Package" on page 78.

The registration package files for the application are grouped beneath a directory called the application root, or *app_root*. The *app_root* directory used for the desktop configuration files can be the same directory as the application's installation *app_root* or some other location.

For example, suppose an application is installed under a directory `/usr/BTE`. This same directory could be used as the *app_root* for the desktop configuration files. However, if you are integrating an existing non-desktop smart application, it is recommended that you create a different desktop *app_root* directory. This will prevent the configuration files you create from being overwritten when you update the application.

For example, a system administrator might want to create a directory `/etc/desktop_approots/BTE` as the desktop *app_root* directory.

Step 3: Creating the Registration Package Directories

Note – For an example of creating the registration package directories for an application, see Step 3 of "Example of Creating a Registration Package" on page 79.

The registration package is the group of desktop configuration files used by the desktop to provide a graphical interface for the application.

Registration Package Contents

The desktop configuration files include:

- Action and data type definition files
- Icon image files
- An application group directory and its contents
- Optionally: help data files and a Front Panel configuration file

The registration package is gathered under a top-level directory called the application root, or *app_root*.

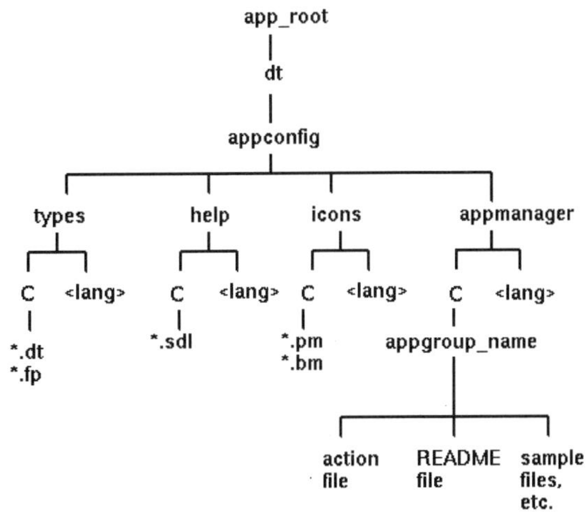

Figure 4-4 A registration package beneath an application root directory

The major categories of configuration fields under the *app_root*/`dt`/`appconfig` directory are:

Subdirectory	Contents
`types`	Action and data type definition files
`help`	Desktop help files
`icons`	Bitmap and pixmap image files used by the application's actions and data types
`appmanager`	The directory and contents that create the application group

Each of the major categories has subdirectories for language-dependent files. Default-language files are placed in the `C` directory.

To Create the Registration Package

- Create these directories. If you are providing language-dependent configuration files, create a separate directory for each language. If you are supplying only one language, put the files in the C directory.
  - *app_root*/dt/appconfig/types/*language*
  - *app_root*/dt/appconfig/help/*language*
  - *app_root*/dt/appconfig/icons/*language*
  - *app_root*/dt/appconfig/appmanager/*language*/*appgroup_name*, where *appgroup_name* is the name of the application group.

  For example, Figure 4-5 shows Application Manager containing an group whose *appgroup_name* is "Media_Tools."

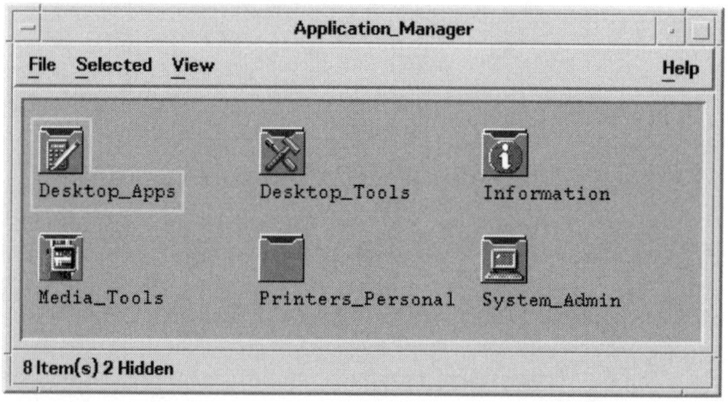

Figure 4-5 Application group at the top level of the Application Manager

The dtappintegrate tool operates only on the desktop configuration files in the types, help, icons, and appmanager directories. The application's binary executable, app-defaults, and message catalog files are administered separately.

Step 4: Creating the Actions and Data Types for the Application

---

Note – For an example of creating the actions and data types for an application, see Step 4 of "Example of Creating a Registration Package" on page 79.

Actions and data types provide a user interface for the application.

- Actions provide a user interface for the command to launch the application.
- Data types provide customized appearance and behavior for the application's data files.

Actions and Data Types Required by an Application

Typical applications require the following action and data type definitions:

- An action that opens the application.
- A data type for the data files of your application. If you create a data type, you will also want to create:
  - An Open action for the data files of your application
  - A Print action for the data files of your application
- A data type for the application group (see "Configuring the Application Group To Use a Unique Icon" on page 70).

For an introduction to how actions and data types are used in the desktop, see Chapter 8, "Introduction to Actions and Data Types."

Location for Action and Data Type Definition Configuration Files

Actions and data types are defined in configuration files. The only naming requirement for files containing action and data type definitions is that they must have a `.dt` suffix. By convention, you may want to name the file *action_name*`.dt` or *application_name*`.dt`.

Place files containing actions and data types under the application root in the directory *app_root*`/dt/appconfig/types/`*language*. The default *language* is `C`.

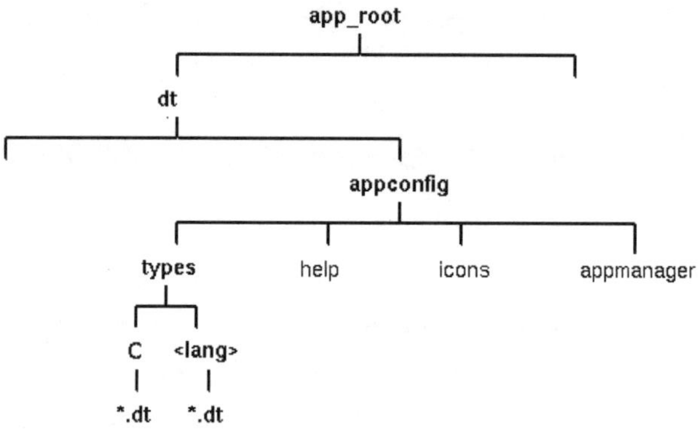

Figure 4-6 Action and data type definition files

Ways to Create Actions and Data Types

You can create action and data type definitions for an application in either of two ways:

- Use the Create Action tool.

  Create Action provides an easy-to-use interface with text fields that you fill in. However, the tool has certain limitations.

- Create the definitions manually.

  This requires you to learn the syntax for creating the definitions, but provides access to the full range of functionality.

▼ To Create Actions and Data Types Using Create Action

This procedure uses the Create Action utility to create an action and data types for the application.

For more information about Create Action, use its online help or see Chapter 9, "Creating Actions and Data Types Using Create Action."

1. Open the Desktop_Apps application group and double-click Create Action.
2. Use Create Action to create the action and data type definitions for the application and its data type.

The configuration file created by Create Action will be written to *HomeDirectory*/.dt/type/*action_name*.dt. The action file (the executable file with the same name as the action) is placed in your home directory.

3. Test the action using the action file created in your home directory.
4. Copy the action definition file *HomeDirectory*/.dt/type/*action_name*.dt to the *app_root*/dt/appconfig/types/*language* directory.
5. After the application group directory has been created (see Section , "Step 7: Creating the Application Group," on page 68), copy the action file *HomeDirectory*/*action_name* to the *app_root*/dt/appconfig/appmanager/*language*/*appgroup_name* directory.

▼ To Create Actions and Data Types Manually

♦ Create a configuration file containing the action and data type definitions for the application.

Action and data type definition files must follow the naming convention *name*.dt.

You can place all your action and data type definitions in one file or distribute them among multiple files. For each file, use a file name that system administrators will easily connect with your application.

Action and data type names must be one word (no embedded spaces). You can use an underscore character. By convention, the first letter of the action or data type name is capitalized. Do not use an existing action name or file name. Use a name that advanced users and system administrators will easily connect with your application.

If you want the application's icon labeled with a different name than the action name, include a LABEL field in the action definition.

For more information about creating actions and data types, see:

- Chapter 8, "Introduction to Actions and Data Types"
- Chapter 9, "Creating Actions and Data Types Using Create Action"
- Chapter 10, "Creating Actions Manually"
- Chapter 11, "Creating Data Types Manually"

Step 5: Putting the Help Files in the Registration Package

Note – For an example of adding help files to a registration package, see Step 5 of "Example of Creating a Registration Package" on page 81.

If the application includes a desktop help volume (a help volume created with the desktop Help Developer's Kit), the help volume master file (`*.sdl`) should be placed in the directory *app_root*`/appconfig/help/`*language*.

Graphics used by the help files are usually placed in a `graphics` subdirectory. The graphics must be located in the same directory relative to the master help volume (`*.sdl`) file as when the help volume was created.

If the application does not provide a help volume, you can create one if you have the Help Developer's Kit.

There are two levels of integration of a help volume:

- Full integration.

  When desktop help is fully integrated, the help volume can be accessed from the application—for example, by on-item help and the Help menu. Full integration involves modification to the application's executables.

- Partial integration.

  When desktop help is partially integrated, it is available from the top level of the Help Manager. However, you cannot access the help volume from the application's windows. You can also provide an action to access the help from the application group. The following example action displays the help volume located in the help master file `MyApp.sdl`:

```
ACTION OpenMyAppHelp
{
  LABEL          MyAppHelp
  ARG_COUNT      0
  TYPE           COMMAND
  WINDOW_TYPE    NO_STDIO
  EXEC_STRING    /usr/dt/bin/dthelpview -helpVolume MyApp
  DESCRIPTION    Displays help for the MyApp application.
}
```

Step 6: Creating Icons for the Application

Note – For an example of creating the icon files for an application, see Step 6 of "Example of Creating a Registration Package" on page 82.

The desktop provides default icons for actions, data types, and application groups. However, you will probably want to create unique icons for the application.

Icons are placed in the directory *app_root*/`dt/appconfig/icons/`*language*.

Icons Required for the Desktop

The application uses these icon images on the desktop:

- **Action icon**. This is the icon the user double-clicks to start your application (actions). It is referenced in the `ICON` field of the action that launches the application.

  Supply three sizes: tiny, medium, and large.

- **Data type icon**. This icon is used to represent the application's data files in File Manager. It is referenced in the `ICON` field of the data type definition.

  If your application supports multiple data types, you should provide a different icon for each data type.

  Supply two sizes: tiny and medium.

- **Application group icon**. This is the icon representing the directory at the top level of the Application Manager. It is referenced in the `ICON` field of the data type definition for the application group. (See "Step 7: Creating the Application Group" on page 68.)

  Supply two sizes: tiny and medium.

You may need to supply both pixmap and bitmap versions of each icon to support color (eight-bit and larger) and monochrome (fewer than eight bits) displays.

Table 4-1 Naming Conventions for Icon Files

Size	Pixel Dimensions	Bitmap Name	Pixmap Name
tiny	16 by 16	*basename*.t.bm	*basename*.t.pm
medium	32 by 32	*basename*.m.bm	*basename*.m.pm
large	48 by 48	*basename*.l.bm	*basename*.l.pm

If you do not provide bitmap files, the desktop maps the color specifications of the pixmap files into black and white. However, this mapping may not produce the appearance you want.

For more information about icons, see "Icon Image Files" on page 201.

Step 7: Creating the Application Group

Note – For an example of creating the application group, see Step 7 of "Example of Creating a Registration Package" on page 82.

Once you have created the action and data type definitions for the application, you must create the configuration files responsible for creating what the user actually sees—the application group and its contents.

The application group is a directory at the top level of the Application Manager (see Figure 4-1 on page 55).

There are three steps to creating the application group:

- Create the application group directory in the registration package.
- Optional: configure the application group to use a unique icon. This involves creating the data type definition for the application group directory.
- Create the contents of the application group.

Creating the Application Group Directory

To create an application group, create the directories in the registration package under `appmanager`, as shown in Figure 4-7.

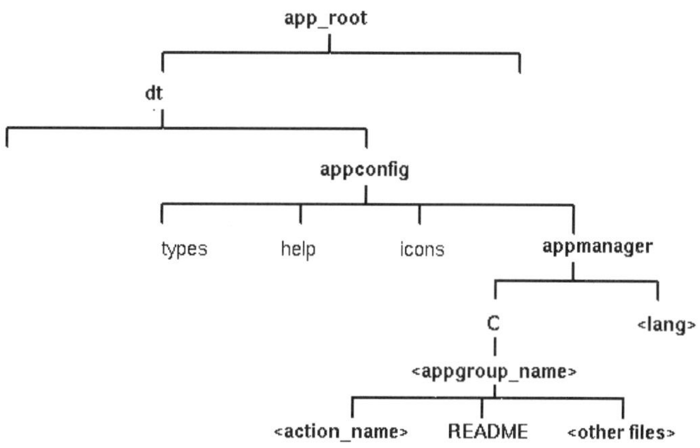

Figure 4-7 The `appmanager` directory

Application Group Name

The <appgroup_name> in Figure 4-7 is the name for the application group.

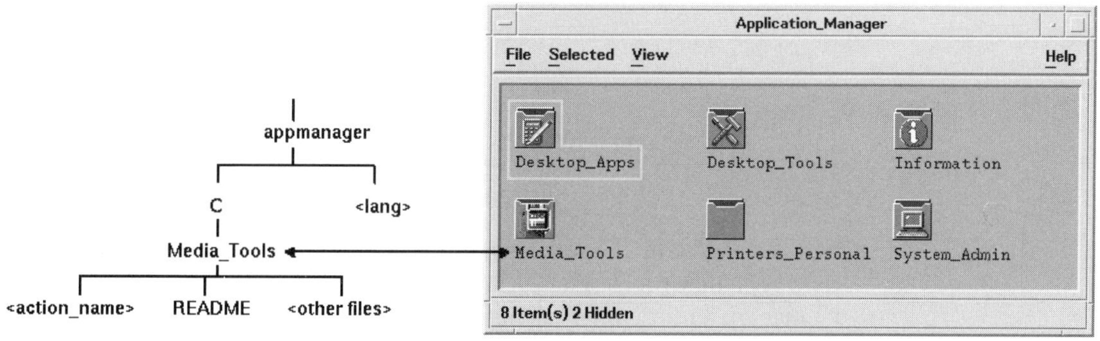

Figure 4-8 The application group name (<appgroup_name>)

The name can be any allowable file (directory) name. Use a name that describes the application.

Configuring the Application Group To Use a Unique Icon

The desktop provides a default application-group icon. However, you will probably want to provide a custom icon.

If you want to provide a unique icon for the application group, you must create:

- A data type for the directory that appears at the top level of Application Manager.
- Open and Print actions for the data type.

For example, suppose you want to create an application group named Media_Tools. The following data type definition, placed in a file *app_root*`/dt/appconfig/types/`*language*`/`*name*`.dt`, assigns a unique icon to the application group icon.

```
DATA_ATTRIBUTES  Media_ToolsAppgroup
{
   ACTIONS       OpenInPlace,OpenNewView
   ICON          MediaTools
   DESCRIPTION   Double-click to open the Media_Tools \
                 application group
}
DATA_CRITERIA           Media_ToolsAppgroupCriteria1
{
   DATA_ATTRIBUTES_NAME Media_ToolsAppgroup
   MODE                 d
   PATH_PATTERN         */appmanager/*/Media_Tools
}
```

The attributes section of the definition specifies the icon to be used. The criteria section of the definition specifies that the data type be defined to any directory named `Media_Tools` that is a subdirectory of a directory named `appmanager`.

Figure 4-9 shows the relationship between the application group name and the data type definition. The `PATH_PATTERN` field in the data type definition connects a unique icon to the application group.

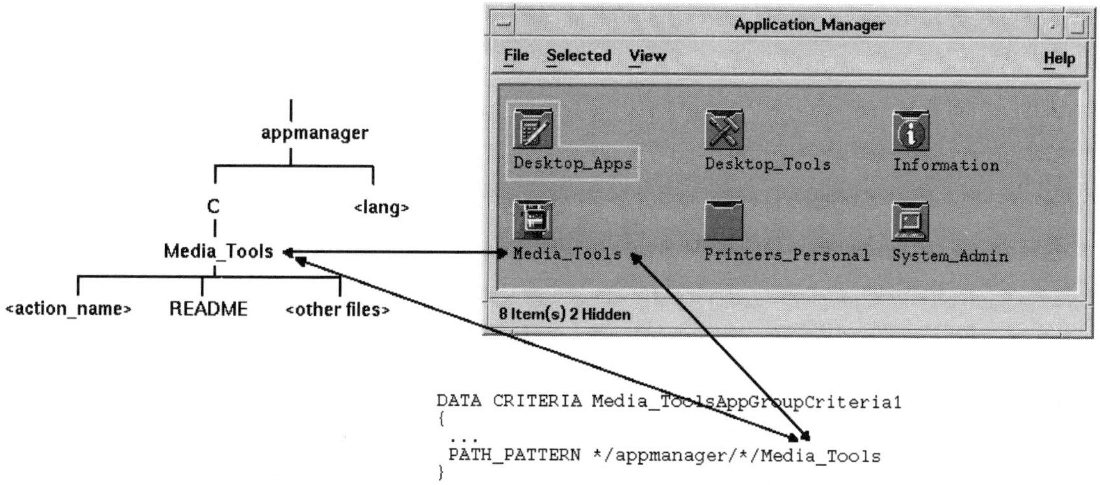

Figure 4-9 How an application group gets a unique icon

You should also create an Open and Print action for the application group data type:

```
ACTION Open
{
    ARG_TYPE    Media_ToolsAppGroup
    TYPE        MAP
    MAP_ACTION  OpenAppGroup
}
ACTION Print
{
    ARG_TYPE    Media_ToolsAppGroup
    TYPE        MAP
    MAP_ACTION  PrintAppGroup
}
```

OpenAppGroup and PrintAppGroup actions are built-in actions defined in `/usr/dt/appconfig/types/`*language*`/dtappman.dt`.

Creating the Contents of the Application Group

The most important item in the application group is an icon to start the application (an action icon). If the application group contains a suite of applications, there is usually an icon for each application.

In addition to one or more action icons, the application group may contain:

- One or more README files
- One or more sample data files
- Templates
- An icon the user can double-click to view help information
- A man page
- A specialized Front Panel control

The application group can contain subdirectories.

Creating the Action File (Application Icon)

The application group should contain an icon that launches the application. If the group supplies a suite of applications, there should be an icon for each one. These icons are called *application icons*, or *action icons*, since they represent an underlying action.

An action icon is created by creating an executable file with the same name as the action it will run:

app_root`/dt/appconfig/appmanager/`*appgroup_name*`/`*action_name*

The file is called an *action file*, because its purpose is to create a visual representation of the underlying action.

For example, if you've created an action named BestTextEditor that runs the BestTextEditor application, you would create an executable file named BestTextEditor. In File Manager and the Application Manager, the action file will use the icon image specified in the action definition.

Figure 4-10 illustrates the relationship between the action definition, action file, and actual entry in the Application Manager window.

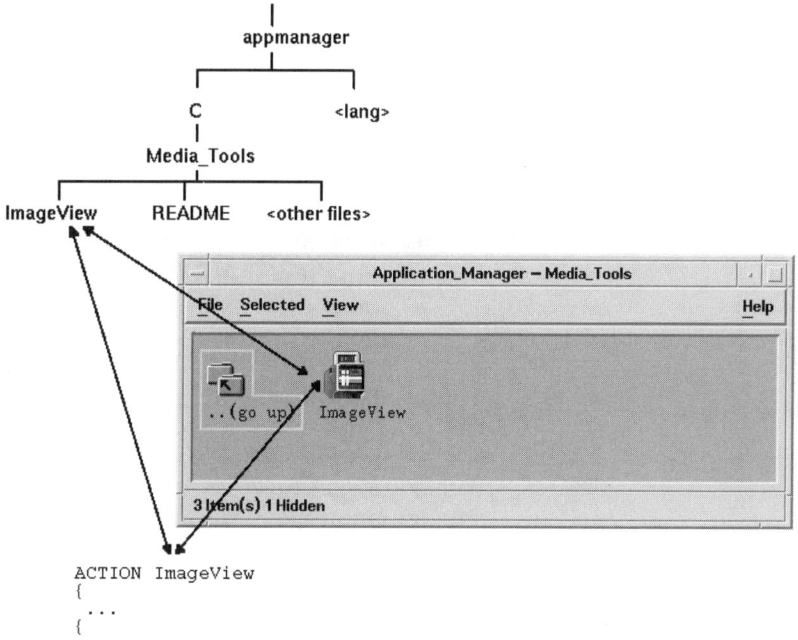

Figure 4-10 The application icon is a file in the application group

Read Me Files

The desktop provides a README data type that you can use for your application's README files. Use one of these naming conventions:

- `README`
- `readme`
- `README.*`
- `Read.*.Me`
- `read.*.me`
- `READ.*.ME`

Creating a Specialized Front Panel Control

In most cases, you do not need to provide a Front Panel control definition; the user can add the application to the Front Panel by dropping the action icon on the Install Icon control in a subpanel.

You might want to create a Front Panel configuration file containing a control definition for your application if you want users to be able to install a control that behaves differently than the action icon—for example, if the control monitors a file and changes appearance when the monitored file changes.

Front Panel configuration files are placed in the *app_root*`/dt/appconfig/types/`*language* directory. The naming convention is *name*`.fp`.

If you supply a configuration file containing a control, the user can add the control to a subpanel by dropping the `*.fp` file on the Install Icon control in the subpanel.

For example, the following definition can be placed in a Front Panel configuration file in the application group. If the user drops this file on an Install Icon control in a subpanel, a control is created in the subpanel that runs a single instance of the BestTextEditor application. If BestTextEditor is already running, the window is moved to the top of the window stack in the current workspace.

```
CONTROL BestTextEditorControl
{
    TYPE            icon
    ICON            BTEFPanel
    PUSH_RECALL     True
    CLIENT_NAME     BTEd
    PUSH_ACTION     BTEditor
    DROP_ACTION     BTEditor
    HELP_STRING     Starts the BestTextEditor application.
}
```

For additional information about creating Front Panel configuration files, see:

- Chapter 13, "Advanced Front Panel Customization"
- The `dtfpfile(4)` man page

Step 8: Registering the Application Using dtappintegrate

Note – For an example of registering an application, see Step 8 of "Example of Creating a Registration Package" on page 83.

Once you've created a registration package under an application root, you are ready to perform the actual application registration.

Application registration creates links between the registration package and the directories located along the desktop search paths (see "How dtappintegrate Integrates Applications" on page 76).

▼ To Register an Application with dtappintegrate

If the application is desktop-smart, `dtappintegrate` is usually run automatically as the final step in the installation process. If it is not run automatically, or if you have created the configuration files to integrate a non-desktop smart application, then you can run `dtappintegrate` manually.

1. Log in as root.
2. Run the command:

   `/usr/dt/bin/dtappintegrate -s` *app_root*

   where *app_root* is the desktop application root directory. For more information, see the `dtappintegrate(1)` man page.
3. Open the Desktop_Tools application group and double-click Reload Applications.
4. Verify that the application is properly registered:

   a. Display the top level of the Application Manager. The new application group should appear in the Application Manager.

   b. Open the application group and double-click the action icon.

Syntax and Options for dtappintegrate

`dtappintegrate -s` *app_root* `[-t` *target_path* `] [-l` *language* `] [-u]`

`-s` *app_root*	Required parameter. Specifies the application root under which the appication has been installed.

`-t` *target_path*	Optional parameter, defaults to the system location `/etc/dt/appconfig`. Specifies the location to which the desktop configuration files are linked. You must use a location on the application search path.
`-l` *language*	Optional parameter, defaults to all languages. Specifies which language-dependent desktop configuration files to integrate.
`-u`	Optional parameter. Un-integrates the application, removing all the links set up during integration.

How dtappintegrate Integrates Applications

The function of `dtappintegrate` is to set up links between the installed files and the locations where the desktop looks for configuration files.

Actions and Data Types

`dtappintegrate` creates symbolic links from the action and data type definition files in the registration package to the system-wide directory along the action database help search path. This is done by creating links from

app_root`/dt/appconfig/types/`*language*`/*.dt`

to

`/etc/dt/appconfig/types/`*language*`/*.dt`

Help Information Files

`dtappintegrate` creates symbolic links from the help files in the registration package to the system-wide directory along the help search path. This is done by creating links from

app_root`/dt/appconfig/help/`*language*`/`*help_file*`.sdl`

to

`/etc/dt/appconfig/help/`*language*`/`*help_file*`.sdl`

Icon Files

`dtappintegrate` creates symbolic links from the icon files in the registration package to the system-wide directory along the icon search path. This is done by creating links from *app_root*/dt/appconfig/icons/*language*/*icon_files*

to

/etc/dt/appconfig/icons/*language*/*icon_files*

Application Group

To place the application group for the application into the top level of Application Manager, dtappintegrate creates a link between the application group directory in the registration package and the system-wide location along the application search path. This is done by creating links from the directory

app_root/dt/appconfig/appmanager/*language*/*appgroup_name*

to

/etc/dt/appconfig/appmanager/*language*/*appgroup_name*

Example of Creating a Registration Package

The following steps create a registration package for an existing, non-desktop smart application named BestTextEditor.

Information You Need to Know About "BestTextEditor"

The example assumes the following facts about the BestTextEditor application:

- It was installed into the directory /usr/BTE.
- The user's session language is the default value, C.
- The command line to start BestTextEditor is:

  BTEd {*filename*]

  where *filename* is the name of the data file to open in the new window. BestTextEditor creates its own window—that is, it does not run inside a terminal emulator window.
- BestTextEditor creates and uses two types of data files:
  - Documentation files. They use the naming convention *.bte. BestTextEditor provides a command line for printing its .bte data files. The syntax of this command is:

    BTEPrint [-d *destination*] [-s] *filename*

    where:

`-d` *destination*	Specifies destination printer.
`-s`	Specifies silent printing. The application's print dialog box is not displayed.
filename	Specifies the file to be printed.

- Template files. They use the naming convention `*.tpl`. Template files cannot be printed.

- The existing, non-desktop app-defaults files for BestTextEditor contain resources for interface fonts and foreground and background colors.
- An online help volume for BestTextEditorwas created using the desktop Help Developer's Kit. When the online help volume was built, it used the following source files:

```
.../BTEHelp.htg
.../graphics/BTE1.xwd
.../graphics/BTE2.xwd
```

  and generated the file `.../BTEHelp.sdl`.

Steps to Registering "BestTextEditor"

The following step-wise procedure registers BestTextEditor.

1. **Modify font and color resources.**

   In BestTextEditor's app-defaults file, remove resources that set:
   - Fonts for text.
   - Colors for foreground and background.

2. **Create the application root.**

   Create the directory:

   ```
   /desktop_approots/BTE
   ```

   If you are integrating an existing application, you should create the application root directory elsewhere than in the installation location for the application; otherwise, the configuration files you create may be removed when you update the application.

3. **Create the registration package directories.**

   Create these directories:

```
/desktop_approots/BTE/dt/appconfig/types/C
/desktop_approots/BTE/dt/appconfig/help/C
/desktop_approots/BTE/dt/appconfig/icons/C
/desktop_approots/BTE/dt/appconfig/appmanager/C/BestTextEditor
```

4. **Create the actions and data types for the application.**

   a. Create the configuration file for the action and data type definitions:

```
/desktop_approots/BTE/dt/appconfig/types/C/BTE.dt
```

   b. Create the action definition for running BestTextEditor:

```
ACTION BTEditor
{
   WINDOW_TYPE     NO_STDIO
   ICON            BTERun
   DESCRIPTION     Double-click this icon or drop a BTE data \
                   file on it to run BestTextEditor.
   EXEC_STRING     /usr/BTE/BTEd %Arg_1%
}
```

   c. Create the data type for `*.bte` files:

```
DATA_ATTRIBUTES BTEDataFile
{
   DESCRIPTION     BestTextEditor data file.
   ICON            BTEData
   ACTIONS         Open,Print
}

DATA_CRITERIA BTEDataFileCriteria1
{
   DATA_ATTRIBUTES_NAME   BTEDataFile
   NAME_PATTERN           *.bte
   MODE                   f
}
```

   d. Create the data type for `*.tpl` files:

```
DATA_ATTRIBUTES BTETemplateFile
{
   DESCRIPTION     BestTextEditor template file.
   ICON            BTETempl
   ACTIONS         Open
}
```

```
DATA_CRITERIAL BTETemplateFileCriterial
{
   DATA_ATTRIBUTES_NAME   BTETemplateFile
   NAME_PATTERN           *.tpl
   MODE                   f
}
```

e. Create the Open action for `*.bte` files.

```
ACTION Open
{
   ARG_TYPE    BTEDataFile
   TYPE        MAP
   MAP_ACTION  BTEditor
}
```

f. Create the Print action for `*.bte` files.

Here are simple Print actions that will print the data files. These actions require a value for the LPDEST environment variable and ignore the `-s` print option. (If LPDEST isn't set, the action may fail.)

```
ACTION Print
{
   ARG_TYPE       BTEDataFile
   TYPE           MAP
   MAP_ACTION     BTEPrintData
}

ACTION BTEPrintData
}
   WINDOW_TYPE         NO_STDIO
   EXEC_STRING         BTEPrint -d $LPDEST %Arg_1%
}
```

Here is another version of the BTEPrintData action and an accompanying script. Together, they handle situations where LPDEST is not set or if silent printing is requested.

```
ACTION BTEPrintData
{
   WINDOW_TYPE     NO_STDIO
   EXEC_STRING     /usr/BTE/bin/BTEenvprint %(File)Arg_1%
}
```

The contents of the /usr/BTE/bin/BTEenvprint script is:

```
# BTEenvprint
#!/bin/sh
DEST=""
SILENT=""
if [ $LPDEST ] ; then
   DEST="-d $LPDEST"
fi
BTEPrint $DEST SILENT $1
```

g. Create the Open action for *.tpl files:

```
ACTION Open
{
   ARG_TYPE    BTETemplateFile
   TYPE        MAP
   MAP_ACTION  BTEditor
}
```

h. Create the Print action for *.tpl files:

```
ACTION Print
{
   ARG_TYPES      BTETemplateFile
   TYPE           MAP
   MAP_ACTION     NoPrint
}
```

NoPrint is a built-in action that displays a dialog box telling the user the file cannot be printed.

5. **Put the help files into the registration package.**

a. Place the help files in the following locations:

```
/desktop_approots/BTE/dt/appconfig/help/C/BTEHelp.sdl
/desktop_approots/BTE/dt/appconfig/help/C/graphics/BTE1.xwd
/desktop_approots/BTE/dt/appconfig/help/C/graphics/BTE2.xwd
```

b. Create the file:

/desktop_approots/BTE/dt/appconfig/types/C/BTEhelp.dt.

Put the following action definition in the file:

```
ACTION BTEHelp
{
  WINDOW_TYPE NO_STDIO
  EXEC_STRING /usr/dt/bin/dthelpview -helpVolume \
```

```
                  BTEHelp.sdl
  DESCRIPTION Opens the BestTextEditor help volume.
}
```

6. **Create icons for the application.**

   Use Icon Editor to create the icons. Use these size guidelines:

Name	**Size**
basename.t.pm	16 by 16
basename.m.pm	32 by 32
basename.l.pm	64 by 64

   Create these icon files in the directory `/desktop_approots/BTE/dt/appconfig/icons/C`:

   - Icons to represent the action that runs the application: `BTERun.t.pm`, `BTERun.m.pm`, `BTERun.l.pm`
   - Icons to represent `*.bte` files: `BTEData.t.pm`, `BTEData.m.pm`,
   - Icons to represent `*.tpl` files: `BTETempl.t.pm`, `BTETempl.m.pm`
   - Icons to represent the application group (used in step 7): `BTEApp.t.pm`, `BTEApp.m.pm`

7. **Create the application group.**

   a. If you haven't already done so, create the directory.

   `/desktop_approots/BTE/dt/appconfig/appmanager/C/BestTextEditor`

   b. This step is optional. It provides a unique icon for the application group icon by creating a data type and associated actions for the application group. If you omit this step, the application group will use the default icon.

   Add the following data type and action definitions to the file `/desktop_approots/BTE/dt/appconfig/types/C/BTE.dt`.The data type specifies the icon to be used by the BestTextEditor application group. The actions provide the same Open and Print behavior as the built-in application groups.

```
DATA_ATTRIBUTES BestTextEditorAppGroup
{
   ACTIONS     OpenInPlace,OpenNewView
   ICON        BTEApp
{
```

```
DATA_CRITERIA BestTextEditorAppGroupCriterial
{
  DATA_ATTRIBUTES_NAME   BestTextEditorAppGroup
  MODE                   d
  PATH_PATTERN           */appmanager/*/BestTextEditor
}
ACTION Open
{
  ARG_TYPE    BestTextEditorAppGroup
  TYPE        MAP
  MAP_ACTION  OpenAppGroup
}
ACTION Print
{
  ARG_TYPE    BestTextEditorAppGroup
  TYPE        MAP
  MAP_ACTION  PrintAppGroup
}
```

c. Create an icon in the application group that will start the application. To do this, create the file:

`/desktop_approots/BTE/dt/appconfig/appmanager/C/BestTextEditor/BTEditor`

and make the file executable.

d. Create the action file in the application group that will open the help volume. To do this, create the file:

`/desktop_approots/BTE/dt/appconfig/appmanager/C/BestTextEditor/BTEHelp`

and make the file executable.

e. Put other files into the application group; for example, "read me" files, sample data and template files.

8. **Register the application.**

In a terminal emulator window:

a. Log in as root.

b. Run the command:

`/usr/dt/bin/dtappintegrate -s /desktop_approots/BTE`

c. Open the Desktop_Tools application group and double-click Reload Applications.

Configuring the Desktop in a Network 5

The desktop is designed to work well in a highly networked environment. The architecture of the desktop lets system administrators distribute computing resources throughout the network, including:

- Applications.
- Data files for applications.
- Desktop session services (desktop applications such as Login Manager and File Manager).
- Help services. Help data files can be put on a central help server.

Overview of Desktop Networking

The operating system provides a variety of networking services, including distributed file systems and remote execution. X servers provide additional networking capabilities, including access to remote displays and security services.

The desktop layers a user interface on top of these networking features. The goals of this interface and its underlying architecture are to make networked systems:

- Easier to use. Users can run applications and access data files without worrying about where in the network the applications and data are located.
- Easier to administer. The desktop provides application integration tools and networked search paths that make it easier for systems to locate remote data and applications. In addition the desktop's file-name mapping process makes it easier to administer complex networks containing numerous servers.
- Flexible. While the administration features of the desktop have been designed for certain common network situations, the desktop can accommodate many other customized network configurations.

Types of Networked Desktop Services

Networking lets a user sitting at a particular display access various computing services distributed among other systems, such as:

- The desktop session and its applications—for example, Workspace Manager and File Manager
- Other applications
- Data files

Networking terminology uses the term *server* to describe a system that provides computing services to one or more other systems. When a system receives services from a server, it is called a *client* of that server.

In a complex network, a system may use services located on a number of systems throughout the network. Furthermore, a system may act as a particular type of server (for example, a session server) and may also be a client (for example, of an application server).

Typical Network Situations

From a desktop perspective, a typical network configuration may contain some combination of these major components:

Displays	Where the X server is running
Login/Session servers	Where the desktop applications (Login Manager, Workspace Manager, etc.) run
Application servers	Where other applications run
File servers	Where data used by applications is located

One of the most common network configurations involves systems accessing an application server. Figure 5-1 illustrates a workstation that uses an application server. The X server and desktop session are running on the workstation.

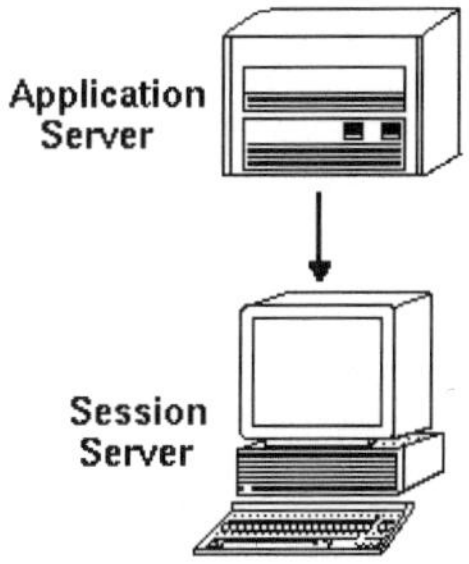

Figure 5-1 Application servers provide services to the desktop session

Networks also frequently use file servers to store large amounts of data. This data may be used by applications running on an application server, or by the desktop applications (for example, File Manager needs access to data files to display them in the File Manager window).

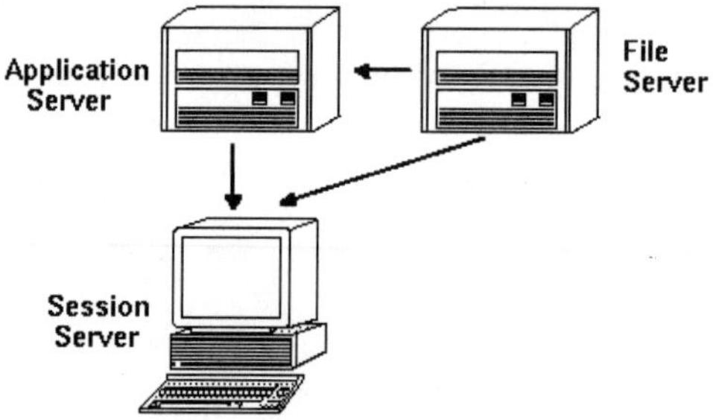

Figure 5-2 Files servers provide data to application servers and session servers

X terminals run the X server and obtain desktop session services from another system.

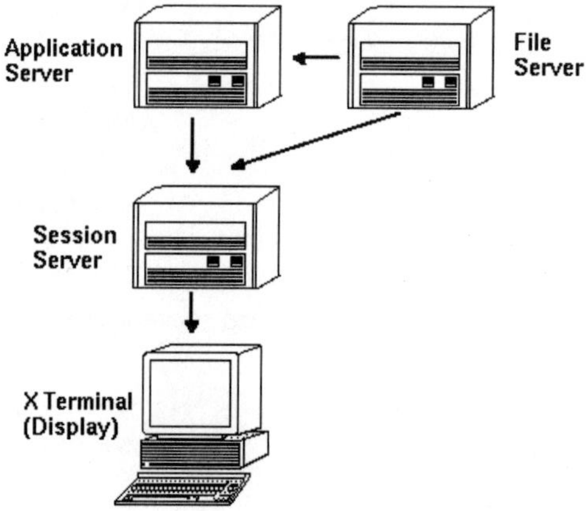

Figure 5-3 X terminals get session services from a session server

Other Networking Situations

The desktop is flexible and can support more complex network configurations. This usually involves making various services, in addition to file servers, available to application servers.

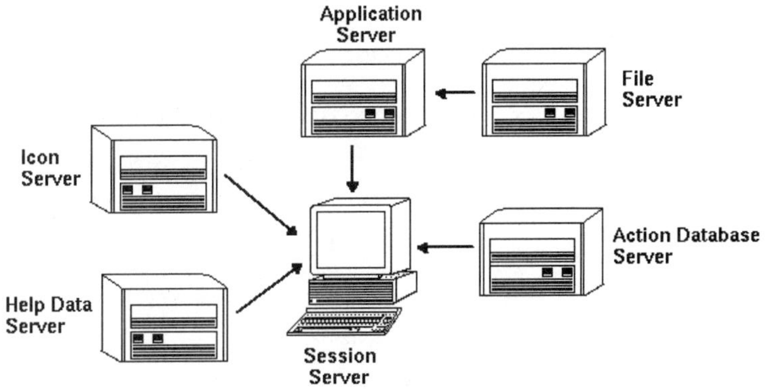

Figure 5-4 Services required by a desktop application server can be distributed

Summary—Types of Servers

Display	The system running the X server.
Login and session server	The system running the desktop session (Login Manager, Session Manager, Window Manager, File Manager, etc.)
Application server	A system on which an application runs. Also called the *execution host*.
File server	A system on which data files for applications are stored
Help server	A system on which help data files are stored
(Action) database server	A system where files containing action and data type definitions are stored
Icon server	A system on which icon files are stored

The network may include additional servers, such as a password server, mail server, video server, etc.

General Steps for Configuring Desktop Networking

There are three general steps for configuring desktop networking:

1. Configure base operating system network services.

   These are the networking services provided by your operating system upon which the desktop depends. See "Configuring Base Operating System Networking for the Desktop" on page 90.

2. Install and configure desktop networking software and services.

   These are the services required by the desktop, regardless of the type of client or server system being set up. See "Configuring Desktop Clients and Servers" on page 93.

3. Configure the particular type of server or client.

   For example, configuring an application server requires different steps than configuring a file server. See "Administering Application Services" on page 99.

Configuring Base Operating System Networking for the Desktop

The desktop requires the following base networking configuration:

- Users must have a login account on the session server and on each system providing desktop services to the session server. The user must have the same user ID and group ID on all client and server systems.
- Systems must have access to remote file systems containing data used by the session and other applications.
- The `lp` print spooler must be configured to access remote printers.
- `sendmail` must be configured for email services.
- X authorization must be set up.

Providing Login Accounts to Users

This section describes the login account requirements for desktop networking.

Providing Login Accounts

Users must have a login account on:

- All systems providing services to the desktop, including application servers, file servers, and systems providing networked printers.
- All session servers the user may access. Usually, session servers are used with X terminals.

Providing Consistent User and Group IDs

UNIX users are identified by a login name and a numeric user ID (UID). In a desktop network, the user should have the same login name and UID on all client and server systems.

UNIX users are also assigned to one or more login groups. Each group has a group name and a numeric group ID (GID). In a desktop network, all systems should use consistent group names and group IDs.

For more information, see the `id(1)` or `id(1M)` man page.

Configuring Distributed File System Access

The desktop uses NFS®, for sharing files between systems. You must identify all the file systems in your network that contain shared files and ensure that they are correctly mounted on all appropriate systems.

Typically, you must provide the following remote file access:

- The user's home directory must be shared by all desktop client and server systems. This is necessary because:
  - The home directory contains data files that must be accessed by applications on remote systems. For example, applications using data files frequently use the home directory as the default data file location.
  - The home directory is the default `dtspcd` authentication directory. For more information about the `dtspcd`, see “Configuring the Subprocess Control Daemon” on page 97.
- If users require access to data files that are not in their home directory, these data files must be shared by all the desktop client and server systems that operate on the data files.

- The desktop installation and configuration directories (`/usr/dt` and `/etc/dt`) must be shared by all the desktop client and server systems so that all of the user's applications access the same desktop configuration files.

Providing a Networked Home Directory

A desktop network works most effectively when users have a single home directory that is shared among all client and server systems on the network.

A networked home directory lets users use different systems in the network without losing personal customizations and configurations. This is because personal customizations and the information required to restore the previous session are saved in subdirectories of the home directory.

A common home directory is also required by:

- The default X authorization mechanism. See "Configuring X Authorization" on page 93.
- The desktop subprocess control daemon, which is involved in launching remote applications, must be able to write to the user's home directory.

File-Name Consistency

You should configure the network so that users can access their data files from all systems using the same name. This is known as providing *file-name consistency,* and is usually accomplished by creating appropriate symbolic links. For example you can configure every system so that each user's home directory is available as `/users/`*login_name* by creating a symbolic link to the actual mount location of the directory.

Configuring Access to Remote Printers

The desktop uses the `lp` print spooler for accessing local or remote printers. See the `lpadmin(1M)` man page for information on configuring the `lp` spooler.

Before attempting to print using the desktop graphical interface, you should test that you can correctly print to all printers using the `lp` command.

It is highly recommended that you use consistent printer device names. For example, if a particular printer is known as `Postscript1` on the system to which it is directly connected, all other systems accessing the printer remotely should also use the name `Postscript1`.

Configuring Electronic Mail

The desktop mailer uses `sendmail` for delivering mail between systems. See the `sendmail(1M)` man page for more information on how to configure email connectivity.

Before attempting to send or receive mail from the desktop, you should test that you can correctly send and receive mail using the `mailx` command.

Configuring X Authorization

The desktop uses the default X mechanism for authorizing remote applications (X clients) to access a local display. The easiest way to configure this is to provide a networked home directory for each user. This ensures that the following requirements are met:

- The user must have read and write permission to the file *HomeDirectory*/`.Xauthority`.
- The `.Xauthority` file on an application server must contain the "magic cookie" for the display on which the application will run.

For more information, see the `X(1)` or `xauth(1)` man pages.

Configuring Desktop Clients and Servers

This section covers network configuration requirements that are specific to the desktop—that is, these capabilities are provided by the desktop rather than by the base operating system.

The section is divided into two parts:

- Configuring login and session services.
- Configuring services required by applications and their data. This includes application, database, icon, file, and help servers and their clients.

Configuring Login and Session Services

A login/session server is a system that supplies desktop services (Login Manager, Session Manager, File Manager, Window Manager, etc.) to a display and X server.

Typically, a session server supplies services to X terminals. However, a network configuration can be set up that concentrates session services on one or more servers that are accessed by both X terminals and workstations.

The Login Manager is the desktop component responsible for supplying login services to other displays. Once the user has logged in, the Session Manager is started for the user.

For information about configuring login/session servers and X terminals, see "Displaying a Login Screen on a Network Display" on page 6.

Configuring Other Application-Related Services

This section covers networking requirements common to the desktop:

- Application servers
- Database servers
- Icon servers
- Help servers

▼ *To Configure Desktop Clients and Servers*

1. Provide the operating system network configurations required by the desktop.

   See "Configuring Base Operating System Networking for the Desktop" on page 90.

2. Install the desktop or the minimum set of files:

   You must install:

   - The entire Common Desktop Environment runtime file sets
   - *Or,* these sets of files: CDE-MIN and CDE-TT

Note – Installation and file sets may differ among vendors.

---

3. Configure the system for the ToolTalk fileame database server daemon `rpc.ttdbserver.`

   This should happen automatically when the desktop is installed. For more information, see "Configuring the ToolTalk Database Server" on page 98.

4. Install and configure the subprocess control daemon (`dtspcd`).

   This should happen automatically when the desktop is installed. For more information, see "Configuring the Subprocess Control Daemon" on page 97.

5. Mount all required remote data.

   Data is considered "remote" when it is located on a system other than the system on which the application using the data is running.

   For example:
   - If an application uses data located on a file server, it must mount those files.
   - If File Manager icons are located on an icon server, the session server must mount those files.
   - If the network uses a help server for desktop help files, the session server and all application servers must mount the help data.

   For more information about mount points, see the next section, "Configuring the Mount Point for Remote File Systems."

Configuring the Mount Point for Remote File Systems

When the desktop passes file names from one system to another, it must transform, or *map*, those file names to names that make sense to the destinition system. This mapping is necessary because a file may be mounted in different locations on the different systems, and therefore must be accessed using different names. For example the file `/projects/big` on `sysA` may be accessed as `/net/sysA/projects/big` on `sysB`.

Requirements for File-Name Mapping

To correctly perform this file-name mapping, one of the following must be true:

- The `mount` command is used to statically mount file systems. These types of static mounts are typically configured in a file such as `/etc/checklist`, `/etc/mnttab`, or `/etc/filesystems`.

For file-name mapping to work correctly between systems, file system mounts must use consistent host names. If a host is known by several names (for example, aliases, or if the host has more than one LAN address that are known by different names), you must use the same name and form of the name for all mounts.

- *Or*, the automounter is used to mount file systems at the default `/net` mount point.
- *Or*, the automounter is used to mount file systems at a location other than `/net` and the DTMOUNTPOINT environment variable is set to indicate the mount point. See the next section, "Setting a Value for DTMOUNTPOINT."

For information about the automounter, see the `automount(1M)` man page.

Setting a Value for DTMOUNTPOINT

You must set the DTMOUNTPOINT environment variable if both of the following conditions are true:

- The automounter is used to mount file systems.
- *And*, remote file systems are mounted at a location other than `/net`.

DTMOUNTPOINT must be set for processes, including:

- The user's desktop processes that are automatically started when the user logs in, such as the Workspace Manager (`dtwm`) and File Manager (`dtfile`)
- System processes such as `rpc.ttdbserver` and `dtspcd` that are started by mechanisms such as `inetd`
- Applications that are started by the desktop on local or remote systems
- Applications that are started by the user from a shell command line

To set DTMOUNTPOINT for all of these processes"

1. Edit the file `/etc/inetd.conf`:

   a. Find the `dtspcd` entry and add:

      `-mount_point` *mount_point*

   b. Find the `rpc.ttdbserver` entry and add:

      `-m` *mount_point*

For example if the automounter is being used with a mount point of /nfs, the entries in /etc/inetd.conf are:

```
dtspc stream tcp nowait root /usr/dt/bin/dtspcd /usr/dt/bin/dtspcd -mount_point /nfs
rpc stream tcp wait root /usr/dt/bin/rpc.ttdbserver 100083 1 rpc.ttdbserver -m /nfs
```

For HP-UX systems, replace wait with swait.

2. Perform the procedure on your system that rereads /etc/inetd.conf. For more information, see the inetd(1M) man page.

3. Set DTMOUNTPOINT such that its value is inherited by user logins.

   This can be done by setting the variable in /etc/dt/config/Xsession.d. For more information on setting environment variables, see "To Set Environment Variables" on page 32.

Configuring the Subprocess Control Daemon

The desktop subprocess control (SPC) service provides client/server command execution.

The desktop subprocess control daemon (dtspcd) is used by the desktop to launch remote applications. It is an inet daemon that accepts requests from remote clients to execute commands. For more information on how to configure inet daemons, see the inetd.conf(1M) man page.

The desktop action invocation library uses the SPC service to invoke remote actions.

To Configure dtspcd

1. Confirm that dtspc is properly registered in both /etc/services and /etc/inetd.conf. See the dtspcd(1M) man page.

2. HP-UX only: Ensure that /usr/adm/inetd.sec is properly configured. See the inetd.sec(4) man page.

SPC Security

Authentication for the subprocess control service is based on file system authentication. The dtspcd must have access to an *authentication directory* that is also mounted by all SPC client systems.

By default the dtspcd authentication directory is the user's home directory. However, you can configure the dtspcd to use a different location by setting the -auth_dir option in the /etc/inetd.conf directory. See the dtspcd(1M) man page for more information.

Because SPC authentication is based on file system authentication, the SPC service is only as secure as your distributed file system. If you are using the desktop in a network where you do not trust the distributed file system, you may wish to disable the dtspcd. To disable the dtspcd, comment out the dtspc entry in /etc/services.

Configuring Environment Variables for Remote Execution

When the desktop uses an action to start an application on a remote system, the user's environment variables are copied to the remote system and placed in the environment of the application.

By default, some of the environment variables are altered before they are copied to the remote system. You can configure both the action invocation component and the subprocess control service of the desktop to perform additional environment variable processing before the variables are placed into the application's environment.

For more information on the default configuration and how to modify it, see the dtactionfile(4) and dtspcdenv(4) man pages.

Configuring the ToolTalk Database Server

One component of ToolTalk is the ToolTalk database server, /usr/dt/bin/rpc.ttdbserver.

The ToolTalk database server is used by the ToolTalk messaging service and for file-name mapping. It is usually registered in /etc/inetd.conf when the desktop is installed and needs no additional configuration.

For more information on the ToolTalk database server and its configuration options, see the rpc.ttdbserver(1M) man page.

Configuring the ToolTalk Message Server

The ToolTalk message server is ttsession. By default, it does not require any configuration; it is started by the Xession script during login.

See the `ttsession` man page for more information on the ToolTalk message server and its configuration options.

Configuring the Calendar Daemon

One component of the Calendar application is the Calendar daemon `rpc.cmsd`. It is usually registered in `/etc/inetd.conf` when the desktop is installed and needs no additional configuration.

For more information on the Calendar daemon and its configuration options, see the `rpc.cmsd(1)` man page.

Administering Application Services

This section covers specific configuration requirements for:

- Application servers and their clients
- Desktop servers that provide special services—database servers, icon servers, and help servers

It also covers networking requirements for two special configurations for networked applications:

- Remote execution hosts
- Applications running across file system mounts

Search Path Environment Variables

The desktop uses a set of environment variables to specify the search path used to find application desktop configuration files such as the actions and data types database, help files, and icon files.

For information on how to use the search path environment variables, see Chapter 7, "Desktop Search Paths," or the `dtenvvar(5)` man page.

Configuring an Application Server and Its Clients

In the standard application server configuration, the application server contains all the binary and configuration files associated with the application, including:

- The application executable(s)
- Standard application configuration files such as app-defaults, message catalogs, and shared libraries for that application.
- Desktop configuration files:
  - Action and data type definition files
  - Icon image files
  - Desktop help data files

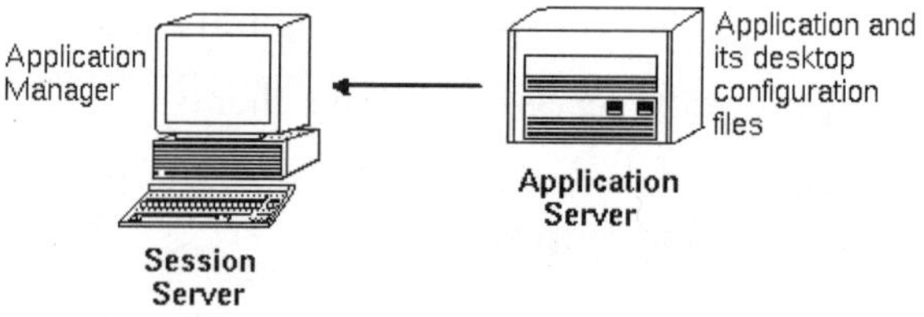

Figure 5-5 Standard application server configuration

▼ *To Configure an Application Server*

1. Provide the operating system network configurations required by the desktop.

   See "Configuring Base Operating System Networking for the Desktop" on page 90.

2. Provide the general desktop configuration required for servers.

   See "To Configure Desktop Clients and Servers" on page 94.

3. Install the application(s).

4. If an application does not automatically register itself, you must perform the registration procedure.

   See Chapter 4, "Registering an Application."

▼ *To Configure the Client of an Application Server*

1. Provide the operating system network configurations required by the desktop.

   See "Configuring Base Operating System Networking for the Desktop" on page 90.

2. Provide the general desktop configuration required for clients.

   See "To Configure Desktop Clients and Servers" on page 94.

3. Add the application server to the application search path on a system-wide or personal basis:

System-wide	Set and export the DTSPSYSAPPHOSTS variable in `/etc/dt/config/Xsession.d/0010.dtpaths`
Personal	Set and export the DTSPUSERAPPHOSTS variable in *HomeDirectory*`/.dtprofile`

For example, the following line in `/etc/dt/config/Xsession.d/0010.dtpaths` adds a system with hostname `SysAAA` and `SysBBB` to the application search path:

```
export DTSPSYSAPPHOSTS=SysAAA:,SysBBB:
```

For more information about setting the application search path, see:

- "Application Search Path" on page 116
- "Setting the Value of a Search Path" on page 115

Configuring Database, Icon, and Help Services

Usually, the action and data type definitions, icons, and help data files associated with an application are installed onto the same system as the application.

For example, consider the typical configuration of help data files:

- The help files for File Manager are usually located on the session server. The desktop finds them because the help search path automatically searches the proper locations on the session server.

- The help files for other applications are usually located on the same application server as the application. The session server finds them because modifying the application search path automatically modifies the help search path.

There may be situations in which you want to place database (actions and data types), help, or icon data elsewhere on the network. For example, if your network uses multiple session servers, you might want to create a help server on which all the help data files for desktop applications (File Manager, Style Manager, etc.) are stored. This conserves disk space because the help files do not need to be duplicated on each session server.

▼ *To Create a Database, Help, or Icon Server*

1. Provide the operating system network configurations required by the desktop.

   See "Configuring Base Operating System Networking for the Desktop" on page 90.

2. Provide the general desktop configuration required for clients.

   See "To Configure Desktop Clients and Servers" on page 94.

3. Install the database, help, or icon files.

   The files can be located anywhere on the system. However, it may be easier to use the following locations, since these are the directories automatically searched when a system has been designated an application server.

   - Database files: `/etc/dt/appconfig/types/`*language*
   - Help files: `/etc/dt/appconfig/help/`*language*
   - Icon files: `/etc/dt/appconfig/icons/`*language*

   If you are setting up a database server, the actions must be written to specify where their commands (`EXEC_STRINGs`) will run. See "Specifying a Remote Execution Host" on page 104.

▼ *To Configure the Session Server to Find a Database, Icon, or Help Server*

1. Provide the operating system network configurations required by the desktop.

   See "Configuring Base Operating System Networking for the Desktop" on page 90.

2. Provide the general desktop configuration required for clients.

   See "To Configure Desktop Clients and Servers" on page 94.

3. Add the database, icon, or help server to the appropriate search path.
   - If you placed the data files in the locations specified in Step 3 of "To Create a Database, Help, or Icon Server," you can modify the application search path.
   - If you placed the data files in other locations, you must modify the specific search path.

     For example, if you placed the help files in directory `/etc/dt/help` on system `SysCCC`, you would add the following line to `/etc/dt/config/Xsession.d/0010.dtpaths`:

     ```
     export DTSPSYSHELP=/net/SysCCC/etc/dt/help
     ```

   For more information about setting search paths, see:
   - "Database (Action/Data Types) Search Path" on page 120
   - "Icon Search Path" on page 122
   - "Help Search Path" on page 123
   - "Setting the Value of a Search Path" on page 115

Special Networked Application Configurations

This section describes how to configure systems to run applications:

- Elsewhere than on the system containing the action—on a remote execution host
- Locally across file system mounts

Specifying a Remote Execution Host

In the typical application server configuration, the action definition is located on the same system as the application executable. However, actions can be written to execute commands on other systems. In this configuration, the system containing the application is called the *execution host*.

The action definition may be located on the session server or on a system that provides action and data type services to the session server—called a *database server* or *database host*.

Action definitions use the EXEC_HOST field to specify where their commands (EXEC_STRINGs) should be run. For example, the following action definition specifies that an xload client be run on a system with host name SysDDD:

```
ACTION XloadSysDDD
{   TYPE            COMMAND
    EXEC_HOST       SysDDD
    EXEC_STRING     /usr/bin/X11/xload -label SysDDD
}
```

If the EXEC_HOST field specifies more than one host name, then the desktop tries to execute the EXEC_STRING on each host in order until it finds one that can run the action. For example, the following EXEC_HOST field specifies that the action should first attempt to run the EXEC_STRING on SysDDD, and, failing this, try SysEEE.

```
    EXEC_HOST       SysDDD,SYSEEE
```

If the EXEC_HOST field is not set for an action, it defaults to the value %DatabaseHost%. The value of %DatabaseHost% is obtained from the database search path.

For example, suppose the database search path has been modified by adding the following line to /etc/dt/config/Xsession.d/0010.dtpaths:

```
export DTSPSYSDATABASEHOSTS=SysAAA:,/net/SysBBB/etc/dt/appconfig/types/C
```

SysAAA is specified using the host-qualified syntax—SysAAA:. An action definition found using this element of the search path sets the database host to SysAAA. However, an action found using the /net/SysBBB... portion of the search path sets the database host to the local system because the syntax does not include the host qualifier.

To Configure the Remote Execution Host

1. Provide the operating system network configurations required by the desktop.

   See "Configuring Base Operating System Networking for the Desktop" on page 90.

2. Provide the general desktop configuration required for servers.

   See "To Configure Desktop Clients and Servers" on page 94.

3. Ensure that the applications are properly installed and configured for local execution.

To Configure the System Containing the Action Definition

1. Provide the operating system network configurations required by the desktop.

   See "Configuring Base Operating System Networking for the Desktop" on page 90.

2. Provide the general desktop configuration required for servers.

   See "To Configure Desktop Clients and Servers" on page 94.

3. Create and install the action definitions and application groups.

   See "Creating Actions that Run Applications on Remote Systems" on page 177 and "Creating and Administering General Application Groups" on page 45.

To Configure the Session Server

1. Provide the operating system network configurations required by the desktop.

   See "Configuring Base Operating System Networking for the Desktop" on page 90.

2. Provide the general desktop configuration required for clients.

   See "To Configure Desktop Clients and Servers" on page 94.

3. Modify the actions search path to include the database host.

   See "Database (Action/Data Types) Search Path" on page 120.

4. Modify the application search path to include the execution host.

   See "Application Search Path" on page 116.

Running Applications Locally

The standard application server configuration runs applications on the application server. Sometimes it is desirable to have the application installed on a remote system but executed locally on the session server.

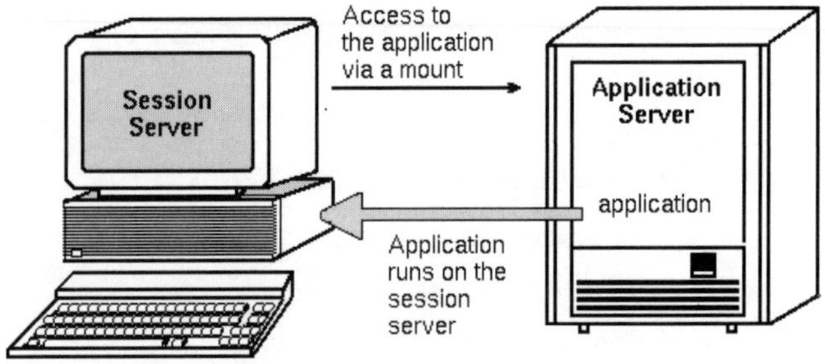

Figure 5-6 Execution across mount points

To Configure the Application Server

No special configuration is required.

To Configure the Session Server

♦ Modify the application search path. Use the local absolute path to the application.

For example, you might use the following variable definition to find an application registered on `sysAAA`:

```
DTSPSYSAPPHOSTS=/net/SysAAA/etc/dt/appconfig/appmanager/C
```

The session server must be able to access the application's configuration files, such as app-defaults, message catalogs, and shared libraries.

Configuring and Administering Printing from the Desktop 6

There are a variety of ways a desktop user can print files. They fall into two major categories: printing from the desktop and printing from an application.

Ways to print from the desktop include:

- Selecting a file in File Manager and choosing Print from the Selected menu or the icon's pop-up menu
- Dragging a file from File Manager to the Front Panel Printer control or the Personal Printers subpanel
- Dragging a file from File Manager to a printer in the Print Manager main window

  To print from an application, use the Print command, usually accessed from a menu or other control within the application's window.

Adding and Deleting Printers

This section contains the procedures for adding and deleting printers from the desktop.

▼ To Add a Printer to the Desktop

1. Add a printer to your system's configuration.

   Follow the instructions in the system administration documentation for your operating system.

2. Run the command:

   ```
   env LANG=language /usr/dt/bin/dtprintinfo -populate
   ```

3. Restart Print Manager or double-click Reload Actions from the Desktop_Tools application group in Application Manager. Verify that the printer shows up.

4. Send mail to your users to let them know they should also restart Print Manager or run Reload Actions.

Each time it is invoked, Print Manager reads the system printers configuration list. If it detects a new printer, it automatically creates a new desktop printer action and icon for that printer. You don't need to do anything else to make the printer appear on the desktop.

▼ To Delete a Printer from the Desktop

1. Remove the printer from your system's configuration.

   Follow the instructions in the system administration documentation for your operating system.

2. Restart Print Manager or double-click Reload Actions from the Desktop_Tools application group in Application Manager. Verify that the printer is gone.

3. Send mail to your users to let them know they should also restart Print Manager or run Reload Actions.

Each time it is invoked, Print Manager reads the system printers configuration list. If it sees that a printer has been removed from the list, it automatically removes that printer's action and icon from Print Manager and File Manager. You don't need to do anything else to delete the printer from the desktop.

Note – Print Manager cannot remove printers from the Front Panel. Therefore, whenever you remove a printer from your configuration, you should send mail to all users on the system telling them to remove any icons of the deleted printer from the Front Panel.

Modifying the Job Update Interval

To change how often the information displayed in Print Manager is updated, modify the job update interval. By default, Print Manager queries printers every thirty seconds for information on their print jobs. You can change how often Print Manager queries the printers by using the Update Interval slider in the Set Options dialog box (displayed by choosing Set Options from the View menu).

Printer Icon Images

When you add a printer, it is automatically assigned the default printer icon. If you have another icon you want to make available for it, place the icon files in `/etc/dt/appconfig/icons/`*language*, or in some other directory along the icon search path. Users can then select this icon to replace the default icon for the printer.

You *must* create a complete set (large, medium, and tiny) of the icons or they will not show up in the icon selector in Print Manager.

For more information about the icon search path, see "Icon Search Path" on page 122.

Icon File Names and Sizes

Icon file-naming requirements are:

base_name.size . type

where:

size l (large), m (medium), t (tiny). For more information about icon sizes, see "Icon Size Conventions" on page 203.

type pm (color pixmap), bm (bitmap).

For example, icon file names for medium and tiny pixmap icons for a color printer might be `ColorPrinter.m.pm` and `ColorPrinter.t.pm`.

Refer to Chapter 12, "Creating Icons for the Desktop for more information on creating icons.

▼ To Globally Change the Icon, Printer Label, or Description of a Printer

You should change global printer properties as soon as you add the printer, before users have modified it using Print Manager. Once a user has modified the printer properties using Print Manager, they will not see the changes you make.

Edit the file `/etc/dt/appconfig/types/`*language*`/`*printer_queue_name*`.dt` with the desired information for the icon, printer label, or description:

1. In the `ICON` field, update *basename* to the new icon base name.
2. In the `LABEL` field, update *labelname* to the new label for the printer.

♦ Update the text In the `DESCRIPTION` field.

This is a good place to put the location of the printer, type of printer, and printer contact. To add more than one line, put a \ at the end of the line. For example:

```
DESCRIPTION    This is a PostScript Printer in Building 1\
               Room 123. Call 555-5555 for problems.
```

Configuring the Default Printer

The default printer is accessed when the user:

- Drops an object on the Front Panel Printer control
- Selects an object in File Manager and chooses Print from the Selected menu or the icon's pop-up menu
- Prints from applications that use the default printer

▼ To Change the Destination for Default Printing

To change the default printer for all users:

1. Open the file `/etc/dt/config/Xsession.d/0010.dtpaths`.

   If `/etc/dt/config/Xsession.d/0010.dtpaths` does not exist, copy it from `/usr/dt/config/Xsession.d/0010.dtpaths`

2. In the `LPDEST=`*printer* line, update *printer* to the new destination for default printing.

   If the line does not exist, add a line `LPDEST=`*printer*, where *printer* is the name of the printer you want to be your default printer.

3. Users need to log out and back in.

To change the default printer for a single user, that user should:

♦ Copy another printer to the Front Panel from the Personal Printers subpanel.

To designate a different printer as the default printer:

1. Go to your home folder and open the file `.dtprofile`.

2. Add or edit a line that sets a value for the LPDEST environment variable:

   `LPDEST=`*printer_device;* `export LPDEST`

   `If you are using csh the syntax is:`

   `setenv LPDEST` *printer_device*

For example, the following line would change the default printer to the printer whose device name is `laser3d`.

```
LPDEST=laser3d; export LPDEST
```

If you are using `csh` the syntax is:

```
setenv LPDEST laser3d
```

Printing Concepts

When a print request is initiated by dropping a file on a printer control, the system proceeds as follows:

1. The system searches the data-type database for the definition of the object dropped.
2. If there is a unique print action for the data type (specified using the `ARG_TYPE` field in the print action), it is used; otherwise, the default print action (`dtlp`) is used. For example, if the file is a PostScript® file, the system uses the Print action for PostScript files. (This action is defined in `/usr/dt/appconfig/types/`*language*`/dt.dt`.) If you used the Create Action tool for this data type, the print command you entered is the unique print action that will be used to print files with this data type.
3. The file is delivered to the printer using the normal UNIX `lp` printing subsystem.

Desktop Search Paths 7

The desktop uses search paths to locate applications and their associated desktop files.

The desktop provides four search paths, described in Table 7-1.

Table 7-1 Desktop Search Paths

Search Path	Description
Applications	Used to locate applications. Application Manager uses the application search path to dynamically populate its top level when a user logs in.
Database	Used to specify additional locations for action and data type definition files (*.dt files) and Front Panel files (*.fp files).
Icons	Used to specify additional locations for icons.
Help data	Used to specify additional locations for desktop help data.

The search paths can include both local and remote directories. Thus, the search paths play an important role in the networking architecture of the desktop. For example, a system finds applications on an application server because that application server is listed in the application search path.

When a search path includes a remote location, you must configure remote file access to the location. For more information, see "Configuring Distributed File System Access" on page 91.

Desktop Search Paths and Their Environment Variables

The desktop search paths are created at login by the desktop utility `dtsearchpath`. The `dtsearchpath` utility uses a combination of environment variables and built-in locations to create the search paths.

The environment variables that `dtsearchpath` reads are called *input variables*. These are variables set by the system administrator or end user. The input variables use the naming convention `DTSP*`.

When dtsearchpath runs at login time, it assembles the values assigned to these variables, adds built-in locations, and creates values for *output variables*. There is an output variable for each search path.

Table 7-2 Desktop Search Path Environment Variables

Search Path For:	Output Environment Variable	System-Wide Input Variable	Personal Input Variable
Applications	DTAPPSEARCHPATH	DTSPSYSAPPHOSTS	DTSPUSERAPPHOSTS
Datatabase[1]	DTDATABASESEARCHPATH	DTSPSYSDATABASEHOSTS	DTSPUSERDATABASEHOSTS
Icons	XMICONSEARCHPATH, XMICONBMSEARCHPATH	DTSPSYSICON	DTSPUSERICON
Help data	DTHELPSEARCHPATH	DTSPSYSHELP	DTSPUSERHELP

1. Actions, data types, and Front Panel definitions

Components use the values of the output variables. For example, Application Manager uses the value of the application search path (DTAPPSEARCHPATH) to locate application groups.

Setting the Value of a Search Path

You can modify the search paths on a system-wide or personal basis. Modifications are done by setting values for the system-wide or personal input variables. Any modifications you make are added to the built-in search path locations.

▼ To See the Current Value for a Search Path (Output Variable)

♦ Use the dtsearchpath command to display the current values for the search paths:

- To obtain the value for the current (login) user, execute:

```
dtsearchpath -v
```

- To obtain the value for a different user, execute:

```
dtsearchpath -u user
```

Search path values include these variables:

%H Used in DTHELPSEARCHPATH. The help volume name.

%B Used in XMICONSEARCHPATH. The base name of an icon file.

%M	Used in XMICONSEARCHPATH. The size of the icon file (.l, .m, .s, .t)
%L	Value of the LANG environment variable.

▼ To Make Personal Modifications to a Search Path

1. Open *HomeDirectory*/.dtprofile for editing.
2. Add or edit a line that defines and exports the personal input variable.

   For example, the following line adds a location to the user's personal application search path:

   ```
   export DTSPUSERAPPHOSTS=/projects1/editors
   ```
3. To make the change take effect, log out and back in.

▼ To Make System-Wide Modifications to a Search Path

1. Log in as root.
2. If the file /etc/dt/config/Xsession.d/0010.dtpaths doesn't exist, create it by copying /usr/dt/config/Xsession.d/0010.dtpaths.
3. Open /etc/dt/config/Xsession.d/0010.paths for editing. Add or edit a line that defines and exports the system-wide input variable.

   For example, the following line adds a location to the system-wide help search path:

   ```
   export DTSPSYSHELP=/applications/helpdata
   ```
4. Inform all users on the system that they must log out and back in for the change to take effect.

Application Search Path

The application search path is the primary search path used by the desktop to locate applications on the local system and on application servers throughout the network.

When locations are added to the application search path, the other search paths (database, icon, and help) are automatically updated to reflect the corresponding locations for that data; thus, the application search path provides relatively simple administration for applications and their desktop configuration files. See "How the Application Search Path Affects the Database, Icon, and Help Search Paths" on page 119.

Default Application Search Path

The default application search path includes personal, system-wide, and built-in locations. The default *language* is `C`.

Personal location	*HomeDirectory*`/.dt/appmanager`
System-wide location	`/etc/dt/appconfig/appmanager/`*language*
Built-in location	`/usr/dt/appconfig/appmanager/`*language*

Application Search Path Environment Variables

The application search path is assembled from the built-in locations and the following input variables:

DTSPSYSAPPHOSTS	System-wide application search path input variable
DTSPUSERAPPHOSTS	Personal application search path input variable

The assembled search path is specified by the output variable DTAPPSEARCHPATH.

Syntax for the Application Search Path Input Variables

The syntax for the variables DTSPSYSAPPHOSTS and DTSPUSERAPPHOSTS is:

VARIABLE=location `[,`*location*`...]`

where *location* can have the syntax:

`/`*path*	Specifies a directory on the local (session server) system. Use this syntax to add a local directory.
hostname`:`	Specifies the system-wide directory `/etc/dt/appconfig/appmanager/`*language* on system *hostname*. Use this syntax to add an application server.

hostname : /*path*	Specifies a directory on the remote system *hostname*.
`localhost:`	The local system-wide location. This keyword is used to alter the precedence of the local system-wide location. See "Changing the Precedence of the System-Wide Local Location" on page 118.

How the Value of the Application Search Path Is Assembled

The value of the application search path (DTAPPSEARCHPATH) is created by assembling the following locations, listed in order of precedence:

- Locations specified using the DTSPUSERAPPHOSTS variable
- The default personal location: *HomeDirectory*/`.dt/appmanager`
- The default location: `/etc/dt/appconfig/appmanager/`*language*
- Locations specified using the DTSPSYSAPPHOSTS variable
- `/usr/dt/appconfig/appmanager/`*language*

The syntax:

hostname:

is expanded to specify the directory `/etc/dt/appconfig/appmanager` on system *hostname*.

Changing the Precedence of the System-Wide Local Location

By default, the local system-wide location (`/etc/dt/appconfig/appmanager/`*language*) has precedence over remote locations. Thus, local application groups have precedence over remote groups with the same name. For example, if both the local and remote systems have Printer application groups (`/etc/dt/appconfig/appmanager/`*language*`/Printers`), the local group is used.

The application search path input variables provide syntax for specifying the precedence of the local system-wide application groups:

`localhost:`

For example, suppose your system must access application servers `SysA`, `SysB`, and `SysC`, and you want the system-wide application groups on `SysB` to have precedence over any local groups with the same name.

The following value for DTSPSYSAPPHOSTS creates this behavior:

```
DTSPSYSAPPHOSTS=SysB:,localhost:,SysA:,SysC:
```

How the Application Search Path Affects the Database, Icon, and Help Search Paths

Additions to the application search path automatically add corresponding locations to the database, icon, and help search paths. This provides the ability to add an application server to a search path by setting only the application search path input variable.

For example, if you set DTSPSYSAPPHOSTS as follows:

```
export DTSPSYSAPPHOSTS=servera:
```

then the following search paths are affected:

Search Path	Directory Added to Search Path
Applications	`servera:/etc/dt/appconfig/appmanager/`*language*
Database	`servera:/etc/dt/appconfig/types/`*language*
Icon	`servera:/etc/dt/appconfig/icons/`*language*
Help	`servera:/etc/dt/appconfig/help/`*language*

Similarly, if you set DTSPSYSAPPHOSTS as follows:

```
export DTSPSYSAPPHOSTS=/projects1/apps
```

then the following search paths are affected:

Search Path	Directory Added to Search Path
Applications	`/projects1/apps/appmanager/`*language*
Database	`/projects1/apps/types/`*language*
Icon	`/projects1/apps/icons/`*language*
Help	`/projects1/apps/help/`*language*

Database (Action/Data Types) Search Path

The database search path directs the desktop to search specified locations for files containing:

- Action and data type definitions (`*.dt` files)
- Front Panel definitions (`*.fp` files).

You may need to modify the database search path when you create a database server, or when you add a local location for database files.

Default Database Search Path

The default database search path includes personal, system-wide, and built-in locations. The default *language* is `C`.

Personal location	*HomeDirectory*`/.dt/types`
System-wide location	`/etc/dt/appconfig/types/`*language*
Built-in location	`/usr/dt/appconfig/types/`*language*

How the Application Search Path Affects the Database Search Path

When a location is added to the application search path, the appropriate database subdirectory is automatically added to the database search path (see "How the Application Search Path Affects the Database, Icon, and Help Search Paths" on page 119).

For example, if the application server `hosta:` is added to the application search path, the directory `hosta:/etc/dt/appconfig/types/`*language* is automatically added to the database search path.

Database Search Path Environment Variables

The database search path is assembled from the built-in locations and the following input variables:

DTSPSYSDATABASEHOSTS	System-wide database search path input variable
DTSPUSERDATABASEHOSTS	Personal database search path input variable

Use these input variables to specify locations outside the application search path.

The assembled database search path is specified by the output variable DTDATABASESEARCHPATH.

Syntax for the Database Search Path Input Variables

The syntax for the variables DTSPSYSDATABASEHOSTS and DTSPUSERDATABASEHOSTS is:

VARIABLE=location `[,`*location*`...]`

where *location* can have the syntax:

/*path*	Specifies a directory on the local (session server) system. Use this syntax to add a local directory.
hostname:	Specifies the system-wide directory `/etc/dt/appconfig/types/`*language* on system *hostname*.
hostname:/*path*	Specifies a directory on the remote system *hostname*.

How the Database Search Path Is Assembled

The value of the database search path (DTDATABASESEARCHPATH) is created by assembling the following locations, listed in order of precedence:

- Locations specified using the DTSPUSERDATABASEHOSTS variable
- Locations derived from the DTSPUSERAPPHOSTS variable
- The default personal location: *HomeDirectory*`/.dt/types`
- The default location: `/etc/dt/appconfig/types/`*language*
- Locations specified using the DTSPSYSDATABASEHOSTS variable
- Locations derived from the DTSPSYSAPPHOSTS variable
- `/usr/dt/appconfig/types/`*language*

The syntax:

hostname:

is expanded to specify the directory `/etc/dt/appconfig/types` on system *hostname*.

Icon Search Path

The icon search path directs the desktop to search specified locations for files containing bitmap and pixmap image files used by the desktop.

Default Icon Search Path

The default icon search path includes personal, system-wide, and built-in locations. The default *language* is `C`.

Personal location	*HomeDirectory*`/.dt/icons`
System-wide location	`/etc/dt/appconfig/icons/`*language*
Built-in location	`/usr/dt/appconfig/icons/`*language*

How the Application Search Path Affects the Icon Search Path

When a location is added to the application search path, the appropriate icon subdirectory is automatically added to the icon search path (see "How the Application Search Path Affects the Database, Icon, and Help Search Paths" on page 119).

For example, if the application server `hosta:` is added to the application search path, the directory `hosta:/etc/dt/appconfig/icons/`*language* is automatically added to the icon search path.

Icon Search Path Environment Variables

The database search path is assembled from the built-in locations and the following input variables:

DTSPSYSICON	System-wide icon search path input variable
DTSPUSERICON	Personal icon search path input variable

Use these input variables to specify locations outside the application search path.

The assembled database search path is specified by two output variables:

XMICONSEARCHPATH	Used by color displays
XMICONBMSEARCHPATH	Used by monochrome displays

Syntax for the Icon Search Path Input Variables

The syntax for the variables DTSPSYSICON and DTSPUSERICON is:

VARIABLE=location [,*location*...]

where *location* can have the syntax:

/*path*	Specifies a directory on the local (session server) system. Use this syntax to add a local directory.

To specify a location on another system, use its network file name—for example, `/nfs/servera/projects/icons`.

How the Icon Search Path Is Assembled

The value of the icon search path (XMICONSEARCHPATH and XMICONBMSEARCHPATH) is created by assembling the following locations, listed in order of precedence:

- Locations specified using the DTSPUSERICON variable
- Locations derived from the DTSPUSERAPPHOSTS variable
- The default personal location: *HomeDirectory*/`.dt/icons`
- The default location: `/etc/dt/appconfig/icons/`*language*
- Locations specified using the DTSPSYSICON variable
- Locations derived from the DTSPSYSAPPHOSTS variable
- `/usr/dt/appconfig/icons/`*language*

The color and monochrome search paths differ only in the precedence given to pixmap and bitmaps. The XMICONSEARCHPATH variables lists pixmaps before bitmaps; XMICONBMSEARCPATH lists bitmaps before pixmaps.

Help Search Path

The help search path directs the desktop to search specified locations for files containing help information that will be registered on your system.

Default Help Search Path

The default help search path includes personal, system-wide, and built-in locations. The default *language* is `C`.

Personal location	*HomeDirectory*/.dt/help
System-wide location	/etc/dt/appconfig/.dt/help/*language*
Built-in location	/usr/dt/appconfig/help/*language*

How the Application Search Path Affects the Help Search Path

When a location is added to the application search path, the appropriate help subdirectory is automatically added to the help search path (see "How the Application Search Path Affects the Database, Icon, and Help Search Paths" on page 119).

For example, if the application server hosta: is added to the application search path, the directory hosta:/etc/dt/appconfig/help/*language* is automatically added to the help search path.

Help Search Path Environment Variables

The help search path is assembled from the built-in locations and the following input variables:

DTSPSYSHELP	System-wide help search path input variable
DTSPUSERHELP	Personal help search path input variable

Use these input variables to specify locations outside the application search path.

The assembled database search path is specified by the output variable DTHELPSEARCHPATH.

Syntax for the Help Search Path Input Variables

The syntax for the variables DTSPSYSHELP and DTSPUSERHELP is:

VARIABLE=location [,*location*...]

where *location* can have the syntax:

/*path*	Specifies a directory on the local (session server) system. Use this syntax to add a local directory.

To specify a location on another system, use its network file name—for example, /nfs/servera/projects/help.

How the Help Search Path Is Assembled

The value of the help search path (DTHELPSEARCHPATH) is created by assembling the following locations, listed in order of precedence:

- Locations specified using the DTSPUSERHELP variable
- Locations derived from the DTSPUSERAPPHOSTS variable
- The default personal location: *HomeDirectory*`/.dt/help`
- The default location: `/etc/dt/appconfig/help/`*language*
- Locations specified using the DTSPSYSHELP variable
- Locations derived from the DTSPSYSAPPHOSTS variable
- `/usr/dt/appconfig/help/`*language*

Localized Search Paths

The output variables include entries for both localized and default (`C`) locations.

For example, the default application search path is:

HomeDirectory`/.dt/appmanager`
`/etc/dt/appconfig/appmanager/`*language*
`/etc/dt/appconfig/appmanager/C`
`/usr/dt/appconfig/appmanager/`*language*
`/usr/dt/appconfig/appmanager/C`

where *language* is the value of the LANG environment variable.

For each scope (system-wide and built-in), the language-specific location has precedence over the default location.

Introduction to Actions and Data Types

8

Actions and *data types* are powerful components for integrating applications into the desktop. They provide a way to create a user interface for starting applications and manipulating their data files.

Introduction To Actions	*128*
Introduction to Data Types	*135*

This chapter introduces the concepts of actions and data types. It describes:

- Why you may want to create actions and data types for applications.
- How actions and data types are related to each other.
- How actions and data types are related to desktop printing.

See Also

The procedures and rules for creating actions and data types are covered in three chapters in this manual.

- Chapter 9 explains how to create actions and data types using the desktop application Create Action.

  You can use Create Action to create actions and data types for most applications without having to learn the syntax rules for their definitions.

- Chapter 10 and Chapter 11 explain how to create actions and data types manually by creating and editing configuration files.

  It is necessary to create actions and data types manually when you want to use advanced features not supported by Create Action.

Introduction To Actions

Actions are instructions written that automate desktop tasks such as running applications and opening data files. Actions work much like application macros or programming functions. Each action has a name that is used to run the action.

Once you define an action, it can be used to adapt the desktop user interface so that tasks are easier to do. The desktop provides the ability to attach user interface components such as icons, Front Panel controls, and menu items to actions.

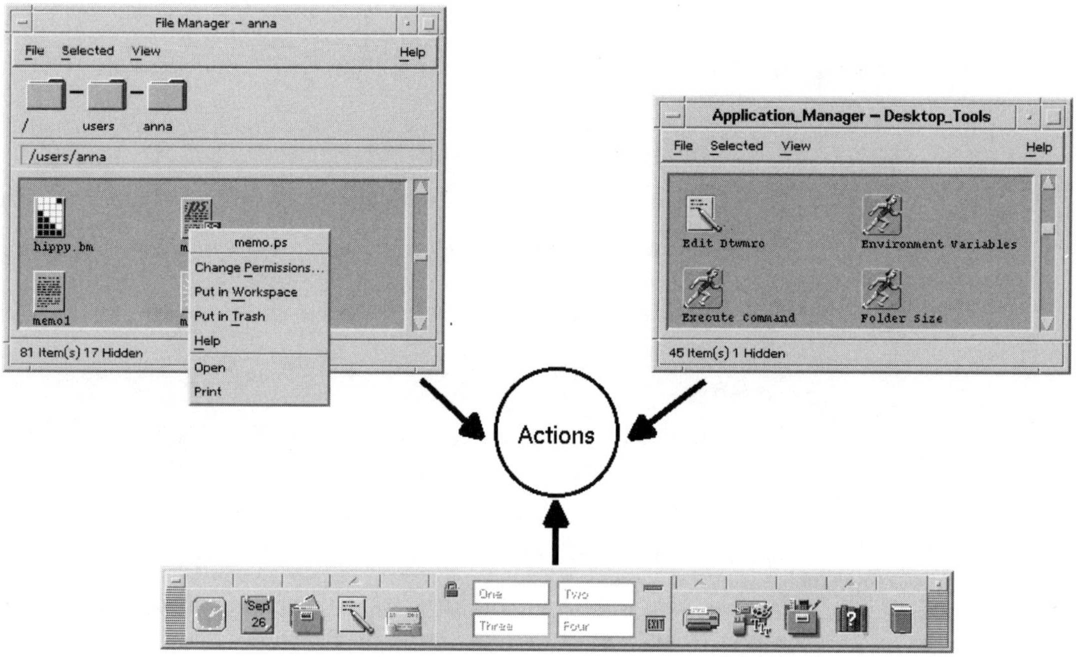

Figure 8-1 Uses for actions

For example, the Desktop_Tools application group in Application Manager contains icons that start various utilities.

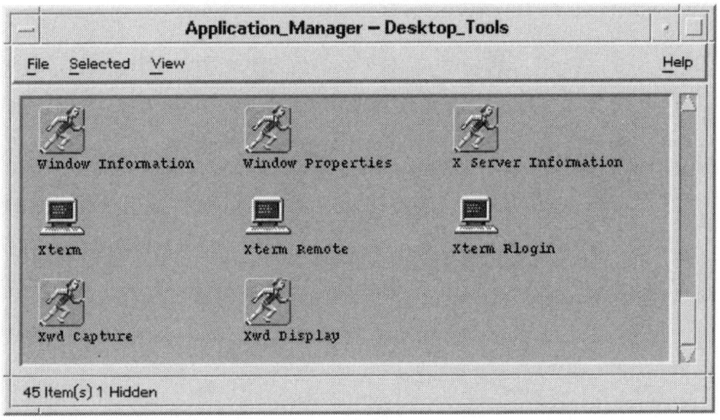

Figure 8-2 Action icons in the Desktop_Tools application group

Each of these icons runs an action when the icon is double-clicked. For example, here's a portion of the definition of the action that runs when the user double-clicks the icon labeled Xwd Display. The action is defined in the configuration file `/usr/dt/appconfig/types/`*language*`/xclients.dt`:

```
ACTION Xwud
{
    LABEL           Xwd Display
    TYPE            COMMAND
    EXEC_STRING     /usr/bin/X11/xwud -noclick -in \
                    %(File)Arg_1"Xwd File To Display:"%
    ...
}
```

The command in the action's `EXEC_STRING` is run when the user double-clicks the icon.

The Front Panel also uses actions. For example, here's a portion of the definition of the control labeled Terminal in the Personal Applications subpanel. The control is defined in the configuration file `/usr/dt/appconfig/types/`*language*`/dtwm.fp`:

```
CONTROL Term
{
    ICON            Fpterm
    LABEL           Terminal
```

```
    PUSH_ACTION     Dtterm
    ...
}
```

The PUSH_ACTION field specifies the action to run when the user clicks the control—in this case, an action named Dtterm.

Another common use for actions is in menus. Data files usually have actions in their Selected menu in File Manager. For example, XWD files (files with names ending in .xwd or .wd) have an Open action that displays the screen image by running the Xwud action.

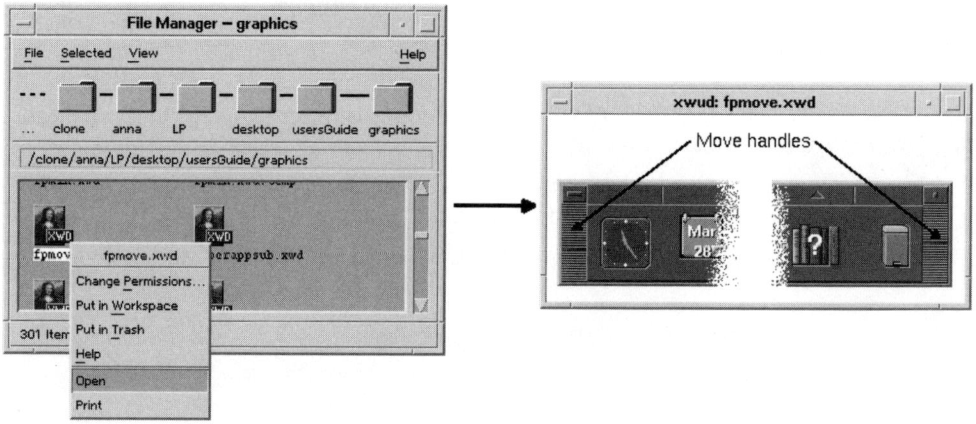

Figure 8-3 Open action for files of data type XWD

The actions in the Selected menu are specified in the data type definition for XWD files. The definition is located in the configuration file /usr/dt/appconfig/types/*language*/xclients.dt.

```
DATA_ATTRIBUTES XWD
{
    ACTIONS         Open,Print
    ICON            Dtxwd
    ...
}
```

The XWD data type, and its associated Open and Print actions, are explained in "How Data Types Connect Data Files to Actions" on page 136.

How Actions Create Icons for Applications

Consider the Xwd Display icon in the Desktop_Tools application group. Double-clicking this icon runs the X client `xwud`. However, this icon does not directly represent the actual `xwud` executable `/usr/bin/X11/xwud`.

The icon labeled Xwd Display appears in the application group because there is a file in that directory named `Xwud` (see Figure 8-4). This file represents an underlying action with the same name—Xwud. In the action definition, the action name is the name following the `ACTION` keyword:

```
ACTION Xwud
{
    LABEL           Xwd Display
    TYPE            COMMAND
    WINDOW_TYPE     NO_STDIO
    EXEC_STRING     /usr/bin/X11/xwud -noclick -in \
                    %(File)Arg_1"Xwd File To Display:"%
    DESCRIPTION     The Xwd Display (Xwud) XwdDisplay action \
                    displays an xwd file that was created using the \
                    Xwd Capture (Xwd) action. It uses \
                    the xwud command.
}
```

The file is called an *action file* because it represents an action. A file is an action file when it is an executable file with the same name as an action. Its icon in Application Manager (or File Manager) is called an *action icon*, or *application icon*, because double-clicking it starts an application.

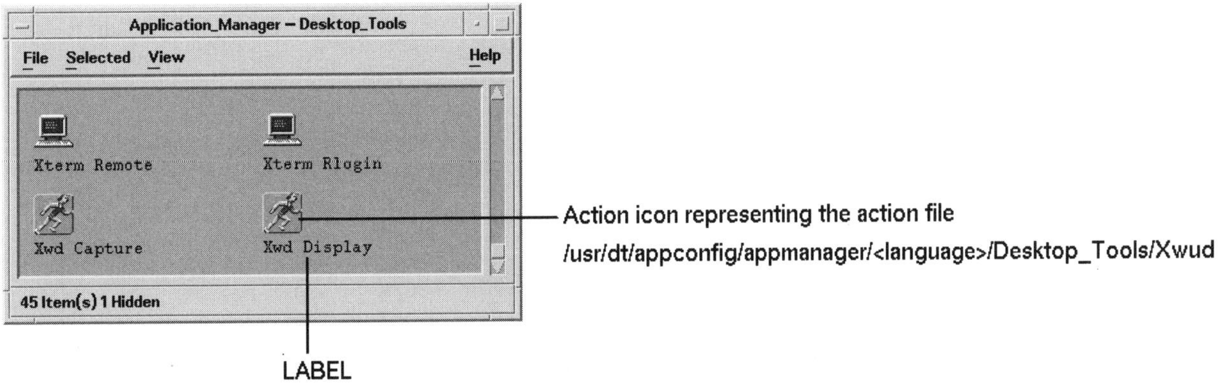

Figure 8-4 Application (action) icon representing an action file

When Application Manager detects an executable file, it looks through the actions database to see if there are any actions whose names match the file name. If a match is found, Application Manager knows that the file is an action file.

The content of the action file is irrelevant; action files usually contain comments describing their desktop function.

Note – The *action file* is not the same as the *action definition file*. The *action file* is a file with the same name as the action. It is used to create the *application icon* in File Manager or Application Manager. The *action definition file* is the file named *name*.dt containing the definition of the action.

Once the desktop determines that a file is an action file, the underlying action definition is used to define the appearance and behavior of the action file.

- The EXEC_STRING field specifies the behavior of the application icon. In the case of the Xwd Display icon, the EXEC_STRING specifies that the action icon runs the xwud X client with certain command-line arguments.
- The LABEL field specifies the label for the application icon.
- The DESCRIPTION field describes the text displayed when the user requests On Item help.
- The Xwud application icon uses the default icon image for actions because its action definition does contain an ICON field to specify a different image.

  In contrast, the icon labeled Compress File uses a different icon image because its underlying action definition contains an ICON field:

  For example:

```
ACTION Compress
  LABEL      Compress File
  ICON       Dtcmprs
  ...
}
```

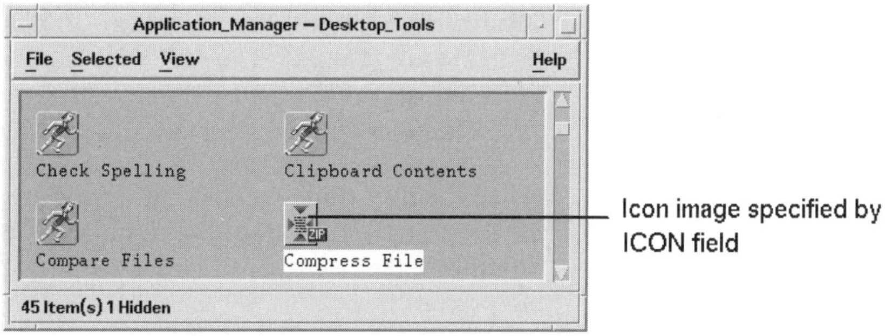

Figure 8-5 Icon image specified by the ICON field in the action definition

The Xwud action is called a *command* action because its definition contains the command (EXEC_STRING) to be run. The TYPE field in the action definition defines the action type.

Initially, the Xwd Display icon appears in the Desktop_Tools application group. However, you can create additional copies of the action icon in any directory for which you have write permission. As long as the Xwud action definition is part of the database, any executable file you create named Xwud will be an action file representing that action, and its icon in File Manager or Application Manager can be used to run the action.

How Actions Use Data Files as Arguments

An *argument* of a command is the thing, usually a file, that the command acts upon. Actions can be written to accept file arguments.

For example, the EXEC_STRING of the Xwud action specifies that a file argument is required:

```
EXEC_STRING     /usr/bin/X11/xwud -noclick -in \
                %(File)Arg_1"Xwd File To Display:"%
```

The term Arg stands for the word *argument.* The syntax Arg_1 means the first argument, and (File) means that the action treats that argument as a file.

The easiest way for the user to provide a file argument is to drop a data file on the application icon. The desktop determines the path of the dropped file and substitutes it into the command line in place of the text between the `%` symbols (`%(File)Arg_1"Xwd File To Display:"%`). Thus, the command that gets executed is:

`/usr/bin/X11/xwud -noclick -in` *file_path*

When the user double-clicks the application icon, the desktop determines from the `EXEC_STRING` that a file argument is required, and displays a dialog box prompting the user to enter a file name or path. In the case of the Xwud action, the prompt is:

```
Xwd File To Display:
```

The file name or path supplied by the user is used as the file argument.

Additional Uses for Actions

In addition to starting applications, actions are used throughout the desktop to create functionality in:

- The Front Panel.

  The definition for a Front Panel control includes fields that specify the action that runs when the user clicks the control or drops a file on it. For more information, see "Defining Front Panel Controls" on page 228.

- Menus.

  The syntax for the Window and Workspace menu definitions allows you to specify the action to be run by a menu item. For more information, see "Workspace Manager Menus" on page 246 and the `dtwmrc(4)` man page.

- Communication between applications.

  An application can be designed to send and receive information using a special type of action called ToolTalk message (`TT_MSG`). `TT_MSG` actions are described in the developer environment documentation for the desktop.

Introduction to Data Types

When the user creates a new data file, the appearance and behavior of the file's icon in File Manager varies depending on the type of data file the user has created. This ability to create custom appearance and behavior for files and directories is provided by the desktop's data typing mechanism.

What Is a Data Type?

A data type is a construct that is defined within the desktop database. For example, here is the definition of the XWD data type. The definition is in the configuration file `/usr/dt/appconfig/types/`*language*`/xclients.dt`:

```
DATA_ATTRIBUTES XWD
{
    ACTIONS          Open,Print
    ICON             Dtxwd
    NAME_TEMPLATE    %s.xwd
    MIME_TYPE        application/octet-stream
    SUNV3_TYPE       xwd-file
    DESCRIPTION      This file contains a graphics image in the XWD \
                     format. These files are typically created by \
                     taking snapshots of windows using the XwdCapture \
                     action. Its data type is named XWD. XWD files \
                     have names ending with '.xwd' or '.wd'.
}

DATA_CRITERIA XWD1
{
    DATA_ATTRIBUTES_NAME    XWD
    MODE                    f
    NAME_PATTERN            *.xwd
}

DATA_CRITERIA XWD2
{
    DATA_ATTRIBUTES_NAME    XWD
    MODE                    f
    NAME_PATTERN            *.wd
}
```

Every data type definition has two parts:

DATA_ATTRIBUTES	Describes the appearance and behavior of the data type.
DATA_CRITERIA,	Specifies the rules (naming or content) for categorizing a file as belonging to that data type.

The DATA_ATTRIBUTES_NAME field connects the criteria to the attributes.

There can be multiple DATA_CRITERIA for a DATA_ATTRIBUTE. For example, the XWD data type has two criteria to specify two different naming criteria (NAME_PATTERN)—names ending with .xwd or .wd.

How Data Types Connect Data Files to Actions

Consider the XWD data type. The user creates an XWD-type file by giving the file one of two file-name suffixes (extensions): .xwd or .wd. The desktop uses the file name as the *criteria* for designating a file as that type.

The XWD data type supplies each file of that data type with:

- A unique icon image that helps users recognize the data files.
- On Item help that tells you about the data type.
- A customized Selected menu in File Manager containing the actions Open and Print. The Open action for XWD files runs the Xwud action.

Running Actions from the Selected Menu

The Selected menu in File Manager is active only when a file or directory is selected. The commands at the bottom of the Selected menu depend on the data type. For example, if an XWD file is selected, the Selected menu includes the items Open and Print.

The ACTIONS field in the data type definition specifies the commands added to the bottom of the data type's Selected menu.

```
DATA_ATTRIBUTES XWD
{
         ACTIONS            Open,Print
         ...
}
```

The contents of the Selected menu depends on the data type. However, many different data types provide an Open action—that is, when you select a file of that particular data type in File Manager and display the Selected menu, you see an Open command.

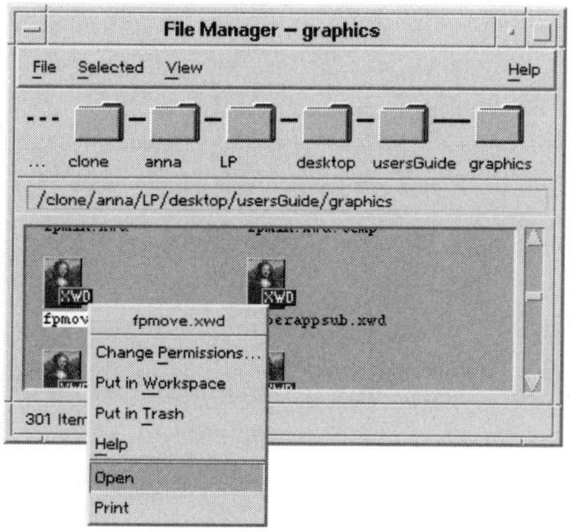

Figure 8-6 The Selected menu for an XWD file

The Open action usually runs the application with which the data file is associated. For example, opening an XWD file runs the Xwud action, which in turn runs the xwud X client to display the screen image. In other words, for the XWD data type, the Open action is synonymous with the Xwud action. Likewise, opening a file of data type TEXTFILE runs the Text Editor, and opening a BM (bitmap) or PM (pixmap) file runs Icon Editor.

The ability to create a variety of Open actions that do different things uses two features of action definitions:

- Action mapping.

  Action mapping lets you create an action that runs another action, rather than directly running a command. For example, you can create an Open action that maps to (runs) the Xwud action.

- Data-type restrictions on an action.

  Action definitions can include an `ARG_TYPE` field that limits the action to certain data types. For example, you can specify that the Open action that maps to the Xwud action applies only to files of data type XWD.

Here is the definition of the action that maps the Open action to the Xwud action for the XWD data type. It is located in the database configuration file /usr/dt/appconfig/types/C/xclients.dt:

```
ACTION Open
{
    LABEL       Open
    ARG_TYPE    XWD
    TYPE        MAP
    MAP_ACTION  Xwud
}
```

The TYPE field specifies that this is a map action; the MAP_ACTION field specifies this action runs the Xwud action. The ARG_TYPE field specifies that this action applies only to files whose data type is XWD.

Compare the previous definition of the Open action to the next definition, which appears in the database file /usr/dt/appconfig/types/C/dt.dt:

```
ACTION Open
{
    LABEL           Open
    ARG_TYPE        BM
    TYPE            MAP
    MAP_ACTION      Dticon
}
```

This definition applies to files of data type (ARG_TYPE) BM (bitmap files). The definition maps the Open action to the Dticon action, which runs Icon Editor.

Defining the Double-Click Behavior of the Data Type

The data type's double-click behavior is defined by the first entry in the ACTIONS field. For example, for the XWD data type, the double-click behavior is to run the Open action, which in turn runs the Xwud action.

Dropping a Data File on an Action Icon

When the user drops a data file on an action icon, the system runs the action using that data file as the argument for the action (see "How Actions Use Data Files as Arguments" on page 133).

For example, when an XWD data file is dropped on the Xwd Display icon, the Xwud action is run using the data file argument. This runs the xwud X client with that data file.

Creating Desktop Printing for a Data Type

Desktop printing provides these ways to print a data file:

- Using the Print command, if available, in the File Manager Selected menu.
- Dropping a data file on a desktop printer drop zone (the Front Panel Printer control or a printer icon in Print Manager).

In addition to desktop printing, many applications provide a way to print from within the application.

Desktop printing uses actions named Print. Print, like Open, is an action name that is used for many different types of data. Therefore, Print actions use action mapping and the ARG_TYPE field to customize printing for each data type.

For example, here is the Print action for the XWD data type. The definition is located in /usr/dt/appconfig/types/*language*/xclients.dt:

```
ACTION Print
{
    LABEL           Print
    ARG_TYPE        XWD
    TYPE            MAP
    MAP_ACTION      NoPrint
}
```

This Print action, specific to XWD files, is mapped to a NoPrint action. NoPrint is a special action defined in /usr/dt/appconfig/types/*language*/dt.dt. The NoPrint action displays a dialog box telling the user that this data type cannot be printed.

Compare the XWD Print action with the following Print action for PCL files:

```
ACTION Print
    LABEL       Print
    ARG_TYPE    PCL
    TYPE        MAP
    MAP_ACTION  PrintRaw
}
```

The PrintRaw action, defined in the configuration file `/usr/dt/appconfig/types/`*language*`/print.dt`, contains the command line for printing the PCL files.

```
ACTION PrintRaw
{
    TYPE            COMMAND
    WINDOW_TYPE     NO_STDIO
    EXEC_STRING     /usr/dt/bin/dtlp -w %(File)Arg_1%
}
```

Creating Actions and Data Types Using Create Action 9

Create Action is a tool for creating:

- An action to start an application
- One or more data types for an application's data files
- Actions for opening and printing the application's data files

Create Action is also useful for creating simple actions for running operating system commands and shell scripts.

For reference information, see the `dtcreate(1X)` man page.

What Create Action Does

Create Action includes a main window and a set of dialog boxes for creating an action and its associated data types.

Create Action does the following:

- Creates an action definition that runs a command.

- Creates a file *HomeDirectory*/.dt/types/*action_name*.dt. This file stores the action and data type definitions created for the application.
- Creates an *action file* in the user's home directory. The action file is an executable file with the same name as the action.

  The action file's representation in File Manager is called an *application icon* because double-clicking it starts the application.

  Optionally, you can make the action icon a drop zone by specifying dropable data types when you create the action.
- Creates one or more data types for the application's data files (optional).
- Creates an Open action for each data type.
- Creates a Print action for each data type (optional).
- Reloads the database of actions and data types. This makes the actions and data types take effect immediately.

Limitations of Create Action

Create Action is designed to create actions and data types for running applications. However, actions and data types are very flexible, and include additional functionality that can only be accessed if you create the definitions manually.

For more information, see:

- Chapter 10, "Creating Actions Manually"
- Chapter 11, "Creating Data Types Manually"

Action Limitations

You cannot use Create Action to create the action for an application if any of the following conditions are true:

- The command line requires a non-file argument (parameter).

  For example, you cannot use Create Action to write an action for the command:

  lp -d*device filename*

  where the user has to supply *device* each time the command is executed.

- The application icon must have a different label than the action name.

  For example, you cannot use Create Action to provide a local-language version of an existing action.

- The action requires any of the advanced features of the action database.

  Examples of these advanced features are actions that:
  - Launch commands on systems remote from the action definition
  - Invoke other actions
  - Must be run as a different user (for example, as superuser)
  - Make extensive use of the "map" feature
  - Have very different behaviors, depending on the number of file arguments supplied to the action

Data Type Limitations

You cannot use Create Action to create the data type for an application if any of the following conditions are true:

- The data type must have additional actions associated with it other than Open and Print.
- The Open action for the data type is not the action's command.

  For example, you cannot use Create Action to create the data type that provides a unique icon for the directory representing the application's application group.

Creating an Action and Data Type for an Application with Create Action

There are some things you'll need to know about the application before you run Create Action.

- The command line for starting the application.

  You'll need to know whether the command line includes a required file argument, an optional file argument, or no file argument.

  If the application requires a non-file argument, you cannot use Create Action to create the action.

- The types of data files an application can accept.

Some applications can accept only one type of data. Others (for example, an ASCII editor or graphics editor) can accept multiple data types.

- The way the application identifies its data files.

  This may be a naming convention (for example, file names ending with .doc), and/or may depend on the content of the file. If the application does not use a file-name convention, you can still set one up for the action icon.

- Optional: The command line to print the files

▼ To Create an Action for an Application

1. Double-click Create Action in the Desktop_Apps application group.

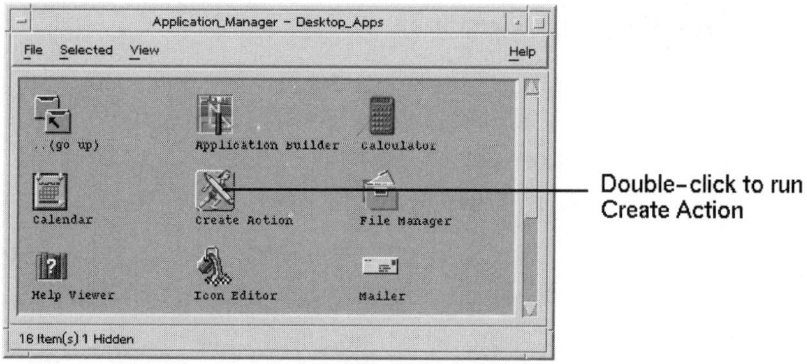

Figure 9-1 Create Action icon in Application Manager

This displays the main Create Action window.

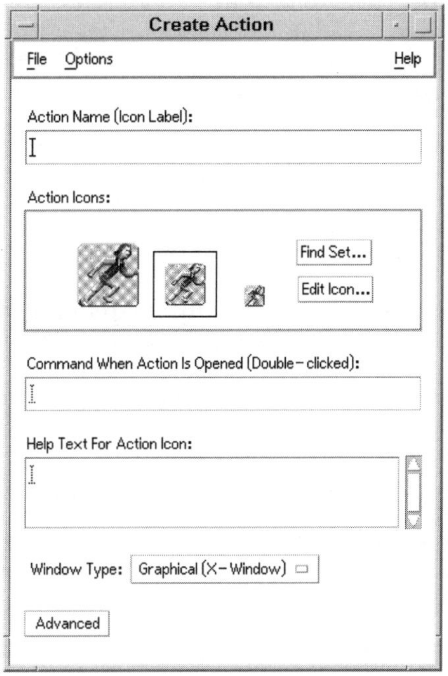

Figure 9-2 Create Action main window

2. Type the name that will label the action icon into the Action Name text field.
3. Use the Action Icons controls to specify the icon for the application. Initially, the default icon is shown.
   - To choose a different, existing icon, click Find Set to display the Find Set dialog box. See "Using the Find Set Dialog Box To Specify an Icon" on page 152.
   - To create new icons, choose Edit Icon to run the Icon Editor.
4. In the Command When Action Icon Is Opened text field, type the command to start the application.

   Use the syntax $*n* for a file argument; for example:

```
emacs
bitmap $1
diff $1 $2
lp -oraw $1
```

If the command line includes a file argument ($*n*), then the action icon will be a drop zone for files.

The command lines are not passed to a shell unless you explicitly specify the use of a shell. For example, these lines use shell processing:

```
/bin/sh -c 'ps | lp'
/bin/sh -c 'spell $1 | more'
```

5. Type the On Item help text for the action icon into the Help Text For Action Icon text field.

   The text will automatically wrap in the text field. However, these line breaks are not preserved online. If you want to specify a hard line break, use `\n`.

6. Choose the windowing support required by the action from the Window Type option menu.

Graphical (X-Window)	The application creates its own window
Terminal (Auto-Close)	The application will run in a terminal emulator window that closes automatically when the user exits the application
Terminal (Manual Close)	The application will run in a terminal emulator window that remains open until the user explicitly closes it
No Output	The application does not produce output to the display

7. Proceed as follows:
   - If your application has data files, and you want to create one or more data types for them, see the next section, "To Create One or More Data Types for an Application."
   - If you do not need to create a data type, save the action by choosing Save from the File menu. Then, test the new action by double-clicking its icon in your home directory.

▼ To Create One or More Data Types for an Application

1. Define the action for the application using the procedure in the previous section, "To Create an Action for an Application."

2. Click the Advanced button in the Create Action window to expand the window.

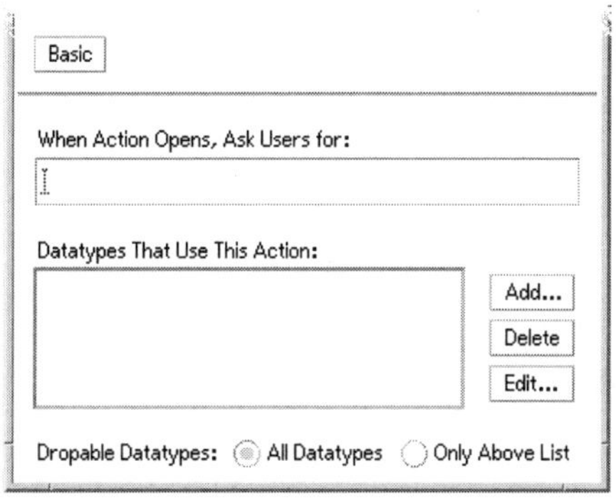

Figure 9-3 Advanced features in the main Create Action window

3. If you want the application icon to prompt for a file argument when the icon is double-clicked, type the text of the prompt into the "When Action Opens, Ask Users for" text field.

   Use these guidelines for this text field:
   - You must use this field if the application's command line has a *required* file argument.
   - You must leave this field blank if the command line does not include a file argument.
   - If the file argument in the application's command line is optional, you have a choice. If you supply the prompt text, the action icon will prompt for the file when double-clicked. If you do not supply the prompt text, the action will be executed with a null string as the file argument.

4. Specify the types of files that the action will accept as arguments:
   - If the action can accept any data type, select All Data Types.
   - If the action can accept only the data type(s) you create for the application, select Only Above List.

   Initially, the Datatypes That Use This Action list is empty. As you create data types for the application, they are added to the list.

5. Click Add beside the Datatypes That Use This Action list box to display the Add Data Type dialog box.

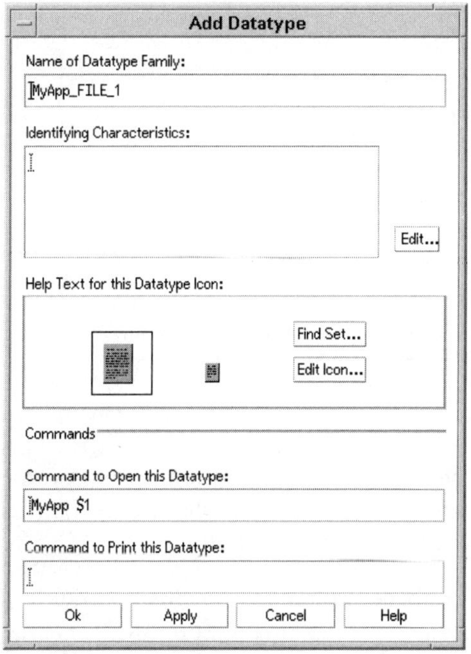

Figure 9-4 Create Action's Add Datatype dialog box

6. Optional: If you don't want to use the default data type name, type a new name for the data type into the Name of Datatype Family text field.

   The name cannot include spaces. The data type name is not visible to application users; it is used in the actions/data types database to identify the data type definition.

7. Click the Edit button beside the Identifying Characteristics box to display the Identifying Characteristics dialog box.

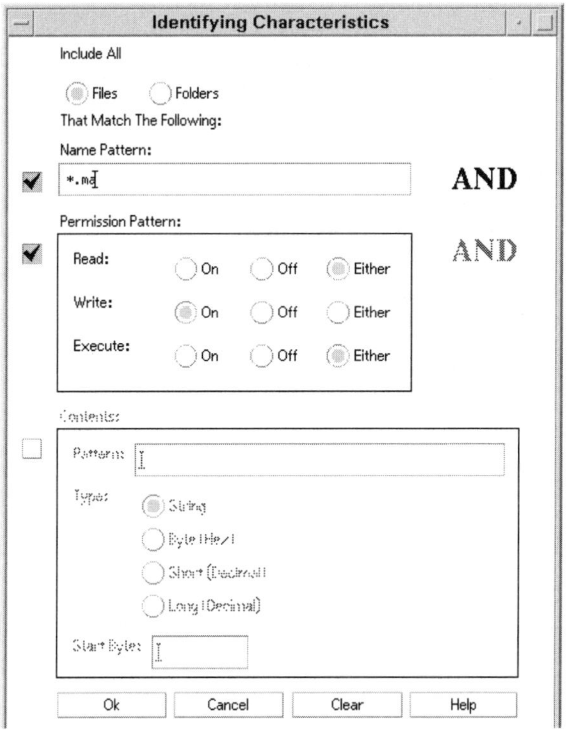

Figure 9-5 Create Action's Identifying Characteristics dialog box

Characteristics of a data type are the criteria used to differentiate the data type from others. You can choose one or more of the following criteria:

Files or Folder	The data type applies only to files or only to folders
Name Pattern	Data typing based on the file name
Permission Pattern	Read, write, execute permissions
Contents	Contents of a specified portion of the file

8. Select whether the data type represents a file or folder.

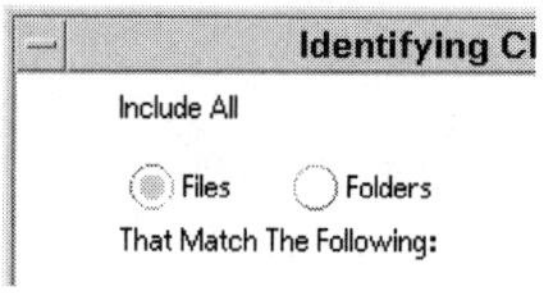

Figure 9-6 Specifying a file or directory characteristic for a data type.

9. If the data typing depends on the name, select the Name Pattern check box and fill in the text field.

AND

Figure 9-7 Specifying the file name characteristic for a data type

You can use * and ? as wildcards:

*	Matches any sequence of characters
?	Matches any single character

10. If the data typing depends on the permissions, select the Permission Pattern check box and select the permissions for the data type.

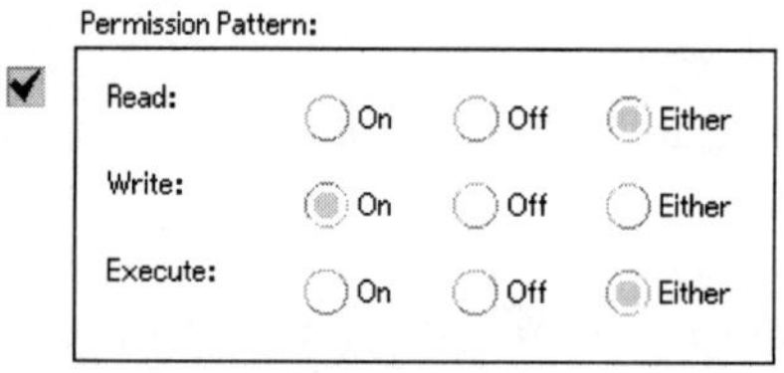

AND

Figure 9-8 Specifying the permission characteristics for a data type

On	The file must have the specified permission
Off	The file must lack the specified permission
Either	The specified permission does not matter

11. If the data typing depends on the contents, select the Contents check box and supply the requested information—Pattern to search for and Type of contents. Optionally, you can supply the byte location where the search should start.

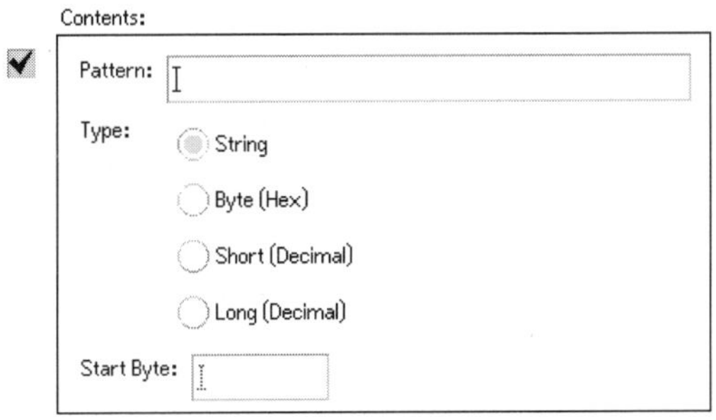

Figure 9-9 Specifying the contents characteristics for a data type

---

Note – Use of content-based data typing may affect the performance of the system.

---

12. Click OK to close the Identifying Characteristics dialog box.

    The characteristics will be displayed in the Identifying Characteristics field using this coding:

    d A directory

    r The file has read permission

    w The file has write permission

    x The file has execute permission

    ! Logical operator NOT

    & Logical operator AND

13. Type the help text for the data files into the Help Text text field.

14. Use the Datatype Icons controls to specify the icon for the application. Initially, the default icon is shown.
    - To choose a different, existing icon, click Find Set to display the Find Set dialog box. See "Using the Find Set Dialog Box To Specify an Icon" on page 152.
    - To create new icons, click Edit Icon to run the Icon Editor.
15. Verify the command in the Command to Open this Datatype text field. This is the command that will be executed when the user double-clicks a data file.
16. Optional: If the application supplies a print command for printing data files from the command line, type the command into the Command to Print this Datatype text field, using the syntax $*n* for a file argument.
17. Do one of the following to save the data type definition:

- Click OK to save the data type and close the Add Datatype dialog box.
- Click Apply to save the data type without closing the Add Datatype dialog box. This let you immediately proceed to define another data type for the action.

Using the Find Set Dialog Box To Specify an Icon

The Find Set dialog box is displayed when you click Find Set in the Create Action main window or in the Add Datatype window. Use the dialog box to specify the icon that will be used for the action or data type.

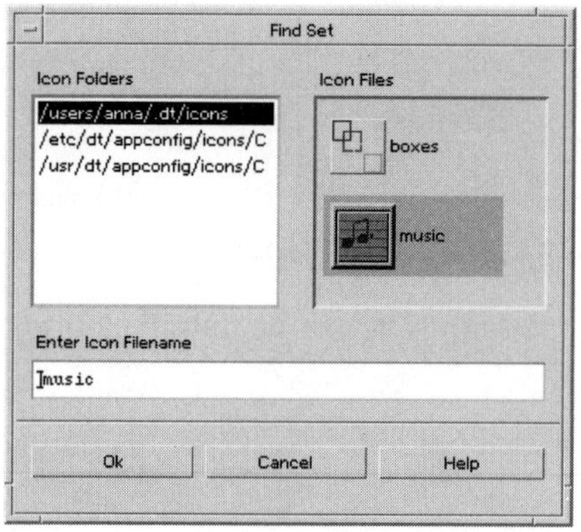

Figure 9-10 Find Set dialog box

The Find Set dialog box lets you specify a set of icon image files located:

- In a directory on the icon search path. The Icon Folders list includes all the directories on the icon search path.
- In a registration package that will be integrated with the desktop using `dtappintegrate`. These icons are not yet located in a directory on the icon search path, but will be placed there by `dtappintegrate`.

Note – The action and data type definitions created using Create Action write out the base name for the icon files (the file name minus the file-name suffixes for size and type). Icons for actions and data types created with Create Action must eventually be placed in directories on the icon search path.

▼ *To Specify a Set of Icons Located on the Icon Search Path*

1. In the Find Set dialog box's Icon Folders list, double-click the folder path containing the icon.

   The Icon Files list will show all the icon files in that folder.

2. In the Icon Files list, click the icon you want to use.

   This places the base name of the icon file in the Enter Icon File name text field.

3. Click OK.

▼ *To Specify an Icon in a Registration Package*

If you are a system administrator or programmer creating a registration package, the icon image files are initially located in a directory in the registration package:

app_root`/dt/appconfig/icons/`*language*

After registration with `dtappintegrate`, the icon files will be copied to `/etc/dt/appconfig/icons/`*language*, which is on the icon search path.

Use this procedure to specify icons that are part of a registration package:

1. In the Find Set dialog box's Enter Icon Filename text field, type the base name of the icon file.

2. Click OK.

   Create Action displays a dialog box to inform you that the icons were not found in directories on the icon search path.

3. In the information dialog box that appears, choose No Change.

Creating Actions Manually 10

There are two ways to create actions:

- Using the Create Action desktop application
- Manually creating an action definition

Creating an action manually requires you to edit a database file. This chapter describes how to manually create action definitions.

See Also

- For an introduction to actions, see Chapter 8, "Introduction to Actions and Data Types."
- For information about using Create Action, see Chapter 9, "Creating Actions and Data Types Using Create Action."
- For reference information about action definitions, see the `dtactionfile(4)` man page.

Reasons You Must Create an Action Manually

There are three basic types of actions:

- `COMMAND`
- `MAP`
- `TT_MSG`

The Create Action tool is designed to create certain types of `COMMAND` and `MAP` actions. All `TT_MSG` actions must be created manually.

For more information, see "Limitations of Create Action" on page 142.

COMMAND Actions

A *command action* executes a command that starts an application or utility, runs a shell script, or executes an operating system command. The definition of the action includes the command to be executed (the `EXEC_STRING`).

The Create Action tool can be used to create the most common types of command actions. However, there may be some situations where you must create the action manually; for example, you must create a `COMMAND` action manually if the action specifies:

- Multiple-file arguments with a different prompt for each argument.
- Action invocation—the ability of actions to invoke other actions.
- Argument-count dependent behavior—the ability to create an action that has very different behaviors for different numbers of file arguments.
- A remote execution host—the ability to run an application on a system other than the one containing the action definition.

- Change of user—the ability to run the action as a different user (for example, to prompt for the root password and then run as root).

MAP Actions

A *map action* is an action that is "mapped" to another action rather than directly specifying a command or ToolTalk message

Mapping provides the ability to specify alternative names for actions. For example, a built-in command action named IconEditor starts Icon Editor. The database also includes an Open action, restricted in the definition to bitmap and pixmap files (by the `ARG_TYPE` field), that is mapped to the IconEditor action. This lets the user start Icon Editor by selecting a bitmap or pixmap file in File Manager and then choosing Open from the Selected menu.

Create Action provides limited mapping for Open and Print actions. All other map actions must be created manually.

TT_MSG (ToolTalk Message) Actions

`TT_MSG` actions send a ToolTalk message. All `TT_MSG` actions must be created manually.

Creating an Action Manually: General Steps

This section explains how to create a configuration file for an action definition.

Configuration Files for Actions

Configuration files containing action definitions must meet these requirements:

- The files must use the naming convention *name*`.dt`
- The files must be located on the database (actions and data types) search path. The default search path is:

Personal actions	*HomeDirectory*`/.dt/types`
System-wide actions	`/etc/dt/appconfig/types/`*language*
Built-in actions	`/usr/dt/appconfig/types/`*language*. You should not use this directory.

For information on modifying the actions/data types search path, see "Setting the Value of a Search Path" on page 115.

To Create an Action Manually

1. Open an existing database file or create a new one. See the previous section, "Configuration Files for Actions."

2. Create the action definition using the syntax:

```
ACTION action_name
{
  TYPE      action_type
  action_field
  ...
}
```

where:

action_name	Name used to run the action.
action_type	COMMAND (default), MAP, or TT_MSG.
action_field	One of the required or optional fields for this type of action. All fields consist of a keyword and a value. Many of the action fields are covered in this chapter. For more information, see the dtactionfile(4) man page.

3. Save the file.

4. If you want the action icon to have a unique image, create the icons for the action. The default location for icons is:
   - Personal icons: *HomeDirectory*/.dt/icons
   - System-wide icons: /etc/dt/appconfig/icons/*language*. The default *language* is C.

   For more information, see "Specifying the Icon Image Used by an Action" on page 163.

5. Double-click Reload Actions in the Desktop_Tools application group.

6. Create an action file for the action. The action file creates an icon in File Manager or Application Manager that represents the action. (If the action is written to start an application, the icon is called an *application icon*.)

To create the action file, create an executable file with the same name as *action_name*. You can put the file in any directory to which you have write permission. You can create as many action files as you like.

Example of Creating a COMMAND Action

The following steps create a personal action that starts a fax application on remote system AppServerA. The command for starting the fax application is:

`/usr/fax/bin/faxcompose [`*filename*`]`

1. Create the file *HomeDirectory*/`.dt/types/Fax.dt`.

2. Put the following action definition into the file:

```
ACTION FaxComposer
{
  TYPE           COMMAND
  ICON           fax
  WINDOW_TYPE    NO_STDIO
  EXEC_STRING    /usr/fax/bin/faxcompose -c %Arg_1%
  EXEC_HOST       AppServerA
  DESCRIPTION     Runs the fax composer
}
```

   The `WINDOW_TYPE` and `EXEC_STRING` fields describe the behavior of the action.

   `WINDOW_TYPE` — The `NO_STDIO` keyword specifies that the action does not have to run in a terminal emulator window.

   See "Specifying the Window Support for the Action" on page 173.

   `EXEC_STRING` — The syntax `%Arg_1%` accepts a dropped file. If the action icon is double-clicked, the action opens an empty fax composer window.

   See "Building the Execution String for a COMMAND Action" on page 166.

3. Save the file.

4. Use Icon Editor to create the following icon image files in the *HomeDirectory*/`.dt/icons` directory:
   - `fax.m.pm`, size 32 by 32 pixels
   - `fax.t.pm`, size 16 by 16 pixels

5. Double-click Reload Actions in the Desktop_Tools application group.

6. Create an executable file named `FaxComposer` in a directory to which you have write permission (for example, your home directory).

Example of Creating a MAP Action

Suppose most of the files you fax are created with Text Editor and are of data type TEXTFILE (files named `*.txt`).

These steps add a "Fax" menu item to the data type's Selected menu.

1. Open the file *HomeDirectory*`/.dt/types/Fax.dt` that was created in the previous example.

2. Add this map action definition to the file:

```
ACTION Fax
{
 ARG_TYPE    TEXTFILE
 TYPE        MAP
 MAP_ACTION  FaxComposer
}
```

3. Save the file.

4. Copy the data attributes definition for TEXTFILE from `/usr/dt/appconfig/types/`*language*`/dtpad.dt` to a new file *HomeDirectory*`/.dt/types/textfile.dt`. Add the Fax action to the `ACTIONS` field.

```
DATA_ATTRIBUTES TEXTFILE
{
 ACTIONS     Open,Print,Fax
 ICON        Dtpenpd
 ...
}
```

5. Save the file.

6. Open Application Manager and double-click Reload Actions in the Desktop_Tools application group.

▼ To Reload the Actions/Data Types Database

In order for new or edited action definitions to take effect, the desktop must reread the database.

♦ Open the Desktop_Tools application group and double-click Reload Actions.

♦ *Or,* execute the command:

```
dtaction ReloadActions
```

ReloadActions is the name of the action whose icon is labeled "Reload Actions."

The actions database is also reread when the user:

- Logs in
- Restarts the Workspace Manager
- Saves an action in the Create Action window by choosing Save from the File menu

Creating an Action File (Icon) for an Action

An *action file* is a file created to provide a visual representation of the action in File Manager or Application Manager.

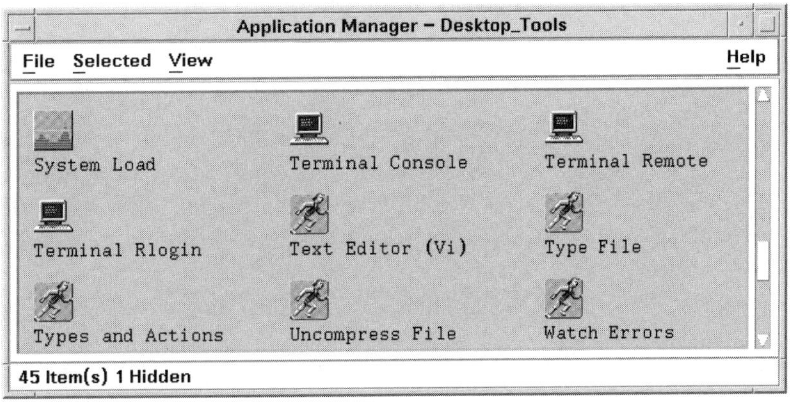

Figure 10-1 *Action files* (also called *action icons* or *application icons*) in Application Manager

Since an action file's icon represents an action, it is sometimes called an *action icon*. If the underlying action starts an application, the action file icon is called an *application icon*.

Double-clicking the action icon runs the action. The action icon may also be a drop zone.

▼ *To Create an Action File (Action Icon)*

♦ Create an executable file with the same name as the action name. The content of the file does not matter.

For example, if the action definition is:

```
ACTION MyFavoriteApp
{
    EXEC_STRING     Mfa -file %Arg_1%
    DESCRIPTION     Runs MyFavoriteApp
    ICON            Mfapp
}
```

then the action file would be an executable file named `MyFavoriteApp`. In File Manager and Application Manager, the `MyFavoriteApp` file would use the icon image `Mfapp.`*size*`.`*type*. Double-clicking `MyFavoriteApp`'s icon would run the action's execution string, and the icon's On Item help would be the contents of the `DESCRIPTION` field (`Runs MyFavoriteApp`).

Action Labels

If the action definition includes the `LABEL` field, the action file will be labeled in File Manager and Application Manager with the contents of this field rather than the file name (*action_name*). For example, if the action definition includes:

```
ACTION MyFavoriteApp
{
    LABEL       Favorite Application
    ...
}
```

then the action icon will be labeled "Favorite Application."

Specifying the Icon Image Used by an Action

Use the ICON field to specify the icon used in File Manager and Application Manager for the action icons created for the action.

If you do not specify an icon, the system uses the default action icon image files /usr/dt/appconfig/icons/*language*/Dtactn.*.

Figure 10-2 Default action icon image

The default action icon can be changed using the resource:

*actionIcon: *icon_file_name*

where *icon_file_name* can be a base name or absolute path.

The value of the ICON field can be:

- A base file name.

  The base file name is the name of the file containing the icon image minus the file-name suffixes for size (m and t) and image type (bm and pm). For example, if files are named GameIcon.m.pm and GameIcon.t.pm, use GameIcon.

  If you use the base file name, the icon files must be placed in a directory on the icon search path:
  - Personal icons: *HomeDirectory*/.dt/icons
  - System-wide icons: /etc/dt/appconfig/icons/*language*

- An absolute path to the icon file, including the full file name.

  You should use the absolute path only if the icon file is not located on the icon search path. For example, if icon file GameIcon.m.pm is placed in the directory /doc/projects, which is not on the icon search path, the value of the ICON field would be /doc/projects/GameIcon.m.pm.

Table 10-1 lists icon sizes you should create and the corresponding file names.

Table 10-1 Icon Names and Sizes for Action Icons

Size in Pixels	Bitmap Name	Pixmap Name
48 by 48	*name*.l.bm	*name*.l.pm
32 by 32	*name*.m.bm	*name*.m.pm
16 by 16	*name*.t.bm	*name*.t.pm

▼ To Modify an Existing Action Definition

You can modify any of the actions available on your system, including built-in actions.

Note – Use caution when modifying the built-in action database. The built-in actions are designed to work well with the desktop applications.

---

1. Locate the definition of the action you want to modify.

   The default locations for action definitions are:
   - Built-in actions: /usr/dt/appconfig/types/*language*
   - System-wide actions: /etc/dt/appconfig/types/*language*
   - Personal actions: *HomeDirectory*/.dt/types

   ,Your system might include additional locations. To see a list of the locations your system uses for actions, execute the command:

   ```
   dtsearchpath -v
   ```

   Your system uses the directories listed under DTDATABASESEARCHPATH.

2. If necessary, copy the text of the action definition to a new or existing file in one of these directories:
   - System-wide actions: /etc/dt/appconfig/types/*language*
   - Personal actions: *HomeDirectory*/.dt/types

   You must copy built-in actions, since you should not edit files in the /usr/dt/appconfig/types/*language* directory.

3. Edit the action definition. When you are done, save the file.

4. Double-click Reload Actions in the Desktop_Tools application group.

Precedence in Action Definitions

When the user invokes an action, the system searches the database for a matching action name. When more than one action exists with that name, the system uses precedence rules to decide which one to use.

- If no other precedence rules apply, the precedence is based on the location of the definition. The following list is ordered from higher to lower precedence:
  - Personal actions (*HomeDirectory*/.dt/types)
  - System-wide local actions (/etc/dt/appconfig/types/*language*)
  - System-wide remote actions (*hostname*:/etc/dt/appconfig/types/*language*). The remote hosts searched are those listed in the application search path.
  - Built-in actions (/usr/dt/appconfig/types/*language*)
- Within a given directory, the *.dt files are read in alphabetical order.
- Actions restricted by ARG_CLASS, ARG_TYPE, ARG_MODE, or ARG_COUNT have precedence over unrestricted actions. (The default for these four fields is *.)

  Where more than one restriction applies, the precedence order from high to low is:
  - ARG_CLASS
  - ARG_TYPE
  - ARG_MODE
  - ARG_COUNT

  Where more than one restricted ARG_COUNT exists, the precedence order from high to low is:
  - Specific integer value *n*
  - $<n$
  - $>n$
  - *

For example, consider the following portions of action definitions:

```
ACTION EditGraphics
# EditGraphics-1
{
    ARG_TYPE        XWD
```

```
    ...
}

ACTION EditGraphics
# EditGraphics-2
{
    ARG_COUNT       0
    ...
}

ACTION EditGraphics
# EditGraphics-3
{
    ARG_TYPE   *
    ...
}
```

Double-clicking the EditGraphics action icon starts EditGraphics-2 because no argument is provided and `ARG_COUNT 0` has precedence. When an XWD-type file argument is provided, EditGraphics-1 is used because it specified the XWD `ARG_TYPE`. EditGraphics-3 is used for all other file arguments.

Building the Execution String for a COMMAND Action

The minimum requirements for a `COMMAND` action are two fields—`ACTION` and `EXEC_STRING`.

```
ACTION action_name
{
    EXEC_STRING execution_string
}
```

The execution string is the most important part of a `COMMAND` action definition. It uses syntax similar to the command line you would execute in a Terminal window but includes additional syntax for handling file and string arguments.

General Features of Execution Strings

Execution strings may include:

- File and non-file arguments
- Shell syntax
- Absolute paths or names of executables

Action Arguments

An argument is information required by a command or application for it to run properly. For example, consider the command line you could use to open a file in Text Editor:

dtpad *filename*

In this command *filename* is a file argument of the dtpad command.

Actions, like applications and commands, can have arguments. There are two types of data that a COMMAND action can use:

- Files
- String data

Using Shells in Execution Strings

The execution string is executed directly, rather than through a shell. However, you can explicitly invoke a shell in the execution string.

For example:

```
EXEC_STRING     \
        /bin/sh -c \
        'tar -tvf %(File)Arg_1% 2>&1 | \${PAGER:-more};\
        echo "\\n*** Select Close from the Window menu to close ***"'
```

Name or Absolute Path of the Executable

If your application is located in a directory listed in the PATH variable, you can use the simple executable name. If the application is elsewhere, you must use the absolute path to the executable file.

Creating an Action that Uses No Arguments

Use the same syntax for the EXEC_STRING that you would use to start the application from a command line.

Examples

- This execution string is part of an action that starts the X client xcutsel.

  ```
  EXEC_STRING xcutsel
  ```

- This execution string starts the client xclock with a digital clock. The command line includes a command-line option but requires no arguments.

  ```
  EXEC_STRING xclock -digital
  ```

Creating an Action that Accepts a Dropped File

Use this syntax for the file argument:

%Arg_*n*%

or

%(File)Arg_*n*%

(File) is optional, since arguments supplied to Arg_*n* are assumed (by default) to be files. (See "Interpreting a File Argument as a String" on page 170 for use of the %(String)Arg_*n*% syntax.)

This syntax lets the user drop a data file object on the action icon to start the action with that file argument. It substitutes the *n*th argument into the command line. The file can be a local or remote file.

Examples

- This execution string executes wc -w using a dropped file as the -load parameter.

  ```
  EXEC_STRING wc -w %Arg_1%
  ```

- This example shows a portion of a definition for an action that works only with directory arguments. When a directory is dropped on the action icon, the action displays a list of all the files in the directory with read-write permission.

  ```
  ACTION  List_Writable_Files
  {
      ARG_TYPE     FOLDER
      EXEC_STRING /bin/sh -c 's -l %Arg_1% | grep rw-'
      ...
  }
  ```

Creating an Action that Prompts for a File Argument

Use this syntax for the file argument:

%(File)"*prompt*"%

This syntax creates an action that displays a prompt for a file name when the user double-clicks the action icon.

For example, this execution string displays a dialog box that prompts for the file argument of the `wc -w` command:

```
EXEC_STRING wc -w %(File)"Count words in file:"%
```

Creating an Action that Accepts a Dropped File or Prompts for One

Use this syntax for the file argument:

`%Arg_`*n*`"`*prompt*`"%`

or

`%(File)Arg_`*n*`"`*prompt*`"%`

This syntax produces an action that:

- Accepts a dropped file as the file argument.
- Displays a dialog box that prompts for a file name when the user double-clicks the action icon.

For example, this execution string performs `lp -oraw` on a dropped file. If the action is started by double-clicking the icon, a dialog box appears prompting for the file name.

```
EXEC_STRING lp -oraw %Arg_1"File to print:"%
```

Creating an Action that Prompts for a Non-File Argument

Use this syntax for the non-file parameter:

`%"`*prompt*`"%`

or

`%(String)"`*prompt*`"%`

`(String)` is optional, since quoted text is interpreted, by default, as string data. This syntax displays a dialog box that prompts for non-file data; do not use this syntax when prompting for a file name.

For example, this execution string runs the `xwd` command and prompts for a value to be added to each pixel:

```
EXEC_STRING xwd -add %"Add value:"% -out %Arg_1"Filename:"%
```

Interpreting a File Argument as a String

Use this syntax for the argument:

```
%(String)Arg_n%
```

For example, this execution string prints a file with a banner containing the file name, using the command `lp -t`*banner filename.*

```
EXEC_STRING lp -t%(String)Arg_1% %(File)Arg_1"File to print:"%
```

Providing Shell Capabilities in an Action

Specify the shell in the execution string:

```
/bin/sh -c 'command'
/bin/ksh -c 'command'
/bin/csh -c 'command'
```

Examples

- This execution string illustrates an action that uses shell piping.

  ```
  EXEC_STRING /bin/sh -c 'ps | lp'
  ```

- This is a more complex execution string that requires shell processing and accepts a file argument.

  ```
  EXEC_STRING /bin/sh -c 'tbl %Arg_1"Man Page:"% | troff -man'
  ```

- This execution string requires that the argument be a compressed file. The action uncompresses the file and prints it using `lp -oraw`.

  ```
  EXEC_STRING  /bin/sh -c 'cat %Arg_1 "File to print:"% | \
               uncompress | lp -oraw'
  ```

- This execution string starts a shell script.

  ```
  EXEC_STRING /usr/local/bin/StartGnuClient
  ```

Creating COMMAND Actions for Multiple File Arguments

There are three ways for actions to handle multiple file arguments:

- The action can be run repreatedly, once for each argument. When an EXEC_STRING contains a single file argument and multiple file arguments are provided by dropping multiple files on the action icon, the action is run separately for each file argument.

For example if multiple file arguments are supplied to the following action definition:

```
ACTION DisplayScreenImage
 EXEC_STRING        xwud -in %Arg_1%
 ...
}
```

the DisplayScreenImage action is run repeatedly.

- The action can use two or more non-interchangeable file arguments. For example:

  `xsetroot -cursor` *cursorfile maskfile*

  requires two unique files in a particular order.

- The action can perform the same command sequentially on each file argument. For example:

  `pr` *file* `[`*file* ...`]`

  will print one or many files in one print job.

Creating an Action for Non-Interchangeable Arguments

Use one of the following syntax conventions:

- If you want the action to prompt for the file names, use this syntax for each file argument:

  `%(File)"`*prompt*`"%`

  Use a different *prompt* string for each argument.

  For example, this execution string prompts for two files.

  ```
  EXEC_STRING  xsetroot -cursor %(File)"Cursor bitmap:"% \
               %(File)"Mask bitmap:"%
  ```

- To accept dropped files, use this syntax for each file argument:

  `%Arg_`*n*`%`

  using different values of *n* for each argument. For example:

  ```
  EXEC_STRING  diff %Arg_1% %Arg_2%
  ```

Creating an Action with Interchangeable File Arguments

Use one of the following syntax conventions:

- To create an action that accepts dropped files and issues a command in the form *command* $file_1$ $file_2$ …, use this syntax for the file arguments:

  `%Args%`

- To create an action that accepts multiple dropped files, or displays a prompt for a single file when double-clicked, use this syntax for the file arguments:

  `%Arg_1"`*prompt*`"% %Args%`

  The action will issue the command in the form: *command* $file_1$ $file_2$ ….

Examples

- This execution string creates an action that executes:

  `pr` $file_1$ $file_2$

  with multiple file arguments.

  ```
  EXEC_STRING pr %Args%
  ```

- This execution string creates an action similar to the previous example, except that the action displays a prompt when double-clicked (no file arguments).

  ```
  EXEC_STRING  pr %Arg_1"File(s) to print:"% %Args%
  ```

Creating an Action for Multiple Dropped Files

To accept multiple dropped file arguments and execute a command line in the form:

command $file_1$ $file_2$ ...

use the syntax:

`%Args%`

Examples

- This execution string executes a script named Checkout for multiple files:

  ```
  EXEC_STRING  /usr/local/bin/Checkout \
               %Arg_1"Check out what file?"% %Args%
  ```

- This execution string executes `lp -oraw` with multiple files:

  ```
  EXEC_STRING  lp -oraw %Arg_1"File to print:"% %Args%
  ```

Windowing Support and Terminal Emulators for COMMAND Actions

There are several ways that `COMMAND` actions support windows on the desktop.

- If the application has its own window, the action can be written to provide no additional window support. This option is also used when an action runs a command that requires no direct user input and has no output.
- If the application must run in a terminal emulator window, the action can be written to open a window and then run the application. There are several terminal options.

Specifying the Window Support for the Action

Use the `WINDOW_TYPE` field to specify the type of windowing support required by the action.

WINDOW_TYPE	Windowing Support Provided
`NO_STDIO`	None. Use `NO_STDIO` if the application has its own window, or if the command has no visible output.
`PERM_TERMINAL`	Permanent terminal emulator window. The action opens a terminal window that remains open until the user explicitly closes it. The user can enter data into the window. Use with commands that take some input, produce some output, then terminate (for example, `ls` *directory*).
`TERMINAL`	Temporary terminal emulator window. The action opens a terminal window that closes as soon as the command is completed. Use with full-screen commands (for example, `vi`).

Specifying Command-Line Options for the Terminal Emulator

Use the `TERM_OPTS` field in the action definition to specify command-line options for the terminal emulator.

For example, the following action prompts for the execution host:

```
ACTION OpenTermOnSystemUserChooses
{
    WINDOW_TYPE     PERM_TERMINAL
    EXEC_HOST       %(String)"Remote terminal on:"%
    TERM_OPTS       -title %(String)"Window title:"%
    EXEC_STRING     $SHELL
}
```

Specifying a Different Default Terminal Emulator

The default terminal emulator used by actions is `dtterm`. You can change this to another terminal emulator. The default terminal emulator is used when the action does not explicitly specify a terminal emulator to use.

The terminal emulator used by actions must have these command-line options:

- `-title` *window_title*
- `-e` *command*

Two resources determine the default terminal emulator used by actions:

- The `localTerminal` resource specifies the terminal emulator used by local applications.

  `*localTerminal:`   *terminal*

  For example:

  `*localTerminal:xterm`

- The `remoteTerminal` resource specifies the terminal emulator used by remote applications.

  `*remoteTerminal:`   *host*`:`*terminal* `[,`*host*`:`*terminal...*`]`

  For example:

  `*remoteTerminal: sysibm1:/usr/bin/xterm,syshp2:/usr/bin/yterm`

Restricting Actions to Certain Arguments

Restricting an action to a particular type of argument refines the action. For example, it is useful to restrict an action that invokes a viewer for PostScript files to only PostScript file arguments; with the restriction, the action will return an error dialog if a non-PostScript file is specified.

You can restrict actions based on:

- The data type of the file argument.
- The number of file arguments—for example, no arguments versus one or more arguments. This provides different drop and double-click behavior for the action icon.
- The read/write mode of the argument.

Restricting an Action to a Specified Data Type

Use the ARG_TYPE field to specify the data types for which the action is valid. Use the data attribute name.

You can enter a list of data types; separate the entries with commas.

For example, the following action definition assumes a Gif data type has been created.

```
ACTION Open_Gif
{
    TYPE            COMMAND
    LABEL           "Display Gif"
    WINDOW_TYPE     NO_STDIO
    ARG_TYPE        Gif
    ICON            xgif
    DESCRIPTION     Displays gif files
    EXEC_STRING     xgif
}
```

Restricting an Action Based on the Number of Arguments

Use the ARG_COUNT field to specify the number of arguments the action can accept. Valid values are:

`*` (Default) Any number of arguments. Other values have precedence over `*`.

n Any non-negative integer, including 0.

>*n* More than *n* arguments.

<*n* Fewer than *n* arguments.

One use for ARG_COUNT is to provide different action icon behavior, depending on whether the user double-clicks the icon or drops a file on it. See the next section, "To Provide Different Double-Click and Drop Behavior."

▼ To Provide Different Double-Click and Drop Behavior

Use this procedure to create an action that accepts a dropped file but does not prompt for a file when the action icon is double-clicked.

1. Create an action definition for the double-click functionality.

   Use the ARG_COUNT field to specify 0 arguments. Use a syntax for the EXEC_STRING that does not accept a dropped argument.

2. Create a second action definition for the drop functionality.

   Use the ARG_COUNT field to specify >0 argument. Use a syntax for the EXEC_STRING that accepts a dropped file.

For example, suppose the following two command lines can be used to start an editor named vedit:

- To start the editor with no file argument:

  `vedit`

- To start the editor with a file argument that is opened as a read-only document:

  `vedit -R` *filename*

The following two actions create drop and double-click functionality for an action named Vedit. The first action has precedence when the database is searched for a match, since ARG_COUNT 0 is more specific than the implied ARG_COUNT * of the drop functionality definition.

```
# Double-click functionality
ACTION Vedit
{
    TYPE            COMMAND
    ARG_COUNT       0
    WINDOW_TYPE     PERM_TERMINAL
    EXEC_STRING     vedit
}

# Drop functionality
ACTION Vedit
{
    TYPE            COMMAND
    WINDOW_TYPE     PERM_TERMINAL
    EXEC_STRING     vedit -R %Arg_1%
}
```

Restricting an Action Based on the Mode of the Argument

Use the ARG_MODE field to specify the read/write mode of the argument. Valid values are:

*	(Default) Any mode
!w	Non-writable
w	Writable

Creating Actions that Run Applications on Remote Systems

When discussing actions and remote execution, there are two terms that are used frequently:

database host	The system containing the action definition
execution host	The system where the executable runs

In most situations, actions and their applications are located on the same system; since the default execution host for an action is the database host, no special syntax is required.

However, when the execution host is different from the database host, the action definition must specify where the execution string should be run.

The ability to locate actions and applications on different systems is part of the client/server architecture of the desktop. For a more in-depth discussion of networked applications, see "Administering Application Services" on page 99.

Creating an Action that Runs a Remote Application

Use the EXEC_HOST field in the action definition to specify the location of the application.

Valid values for EXEC_HOST are:

%DatabaseHost%	The host where the action is defined.
%LocalHost%	The host where the action is invoked (the *session server*).
%DisplayHost%	The host running the X server (not allowed for X terminals).
%SessionHost%	The host where the controlling Login Manager is running.

hostname	The named host. Use this value for environments in which the action should always be invoked on one particular host.
`%"`*prompt*`"%`	Prompts the user for the host name each time the action is invoked.

The default value is `%DatabaseHost%`, `%LocalHost%`. Thus, when the `EXEC_HOST` field is omitted, the action first attempts to run the command on the host containing the action definition. If this fails, the action attempts to run the command on the session server.

Examples

- This field specifies host `ddsyd`:

```
EXEC_HOST   ddsyd
```

- The field prompts for a host name:

```
EXEC_HOST   %"Host containing application:"%
```

- This field specifies that the action will attempt to run the application on the host containing the action definition. If this fails, the action will attempt to run the application on host `ddsyd`.

```
EXEC_HOST   %DatabaseHost%, ddsyd
```

Using Variables in Action and Data Type Definitions

You can include string variables and environment variables in action and data type definition files.

Using String Variables in an Action

A string variable definition remains in effect from the location of the definition to the end of the file. There are no global string variables for the database.

If a string variable and environment variable have the same name, the string variable has precedence.

▼ *To Define a String Variable*

♦ Use the syntax:

`set` *variable_name=value*

Variable names can contain any alphanumeric characters and underscore (_). Each variable definition must be on a separate line.

For example:

```
set Remote_Application_Server=sysapp
set Remote_File_Server=sysdata
```

▼ *To Reference a String Variable*

♦ Use the syntax:

`$[{]`*variable_name*`[}]`

For example:

```
EXEC-HOST   $Remote_Application_Server
CWD         /net/${Remote_File_Server}/doc/project
```

Using Environment Variables in Actions and Data Types

♦ Reference an environment variable using the syntax:

`$[{]`*variable*`[}].`

The variable is expanded (replaced by its value) when the database is loaded. If a string variable and environment variable have the same name, the string variable has precedence.

For example, this execution string prints a file with a banner containing the login name.

```
EXEC-STRING lp -t$LOGNAME %(File)Arg_1%
```

Invoking Actions from a Command Line

The desktop provides the `dtaction` command for running actions from a command line. You can use `dtaction` to run actions from:

- Scripts
- Other actions
- A terminal emulator command line

Syntax of dtaction

```
dtaction [-user user_name] [-execHost hostname] action_name [argument [argument]...]
```

-user *user_name*	Provides the ability to run the action as a different user. If dtaction is invoked by a user other than *user_name*, a prompt is displayed for the password.
-execHost *hostname*	For COMMAND actions only; specifies the host on which the command will be run.
argument	Arguments to the action; usually file arguments.

The dtaction client has additional command-line options. For more information, see the dtaction(1) man page.

Creating an Action that Runs Another Action

Use dtaction in the EXEC_STRING of the action.

For example, the following action uses a built-in action named Spell (the action is labeled "Check Spelling" in Application Manager). The new action runs Text Editor and the Spell action, displaying the spelling errors in a separate terminal emulator window.

```
ACTION EditAndSpell
{
    WINDOW_TYPE     NO_STDIO
    EXEC_STRING     /bin/sh -c 'dtaction Spell \
                    %Arg_1"File:"%; dtpad %Arg_1%'
}
```

Creating an Action that Runs as a Different User

Use the following syntax in the EXEC_STRING:

```
EXEC_STRING   dtaction -user user_name action_name [file_argument]
```

The new user (*user_name*) must have display access to the system through one of the following mechanisms:

- Read permission on the login user's .Xauthority file
- *Or,* xhost permission

For example, the following two actions provide the ability to become root and edit an app-defaults file.

```
ACTION AppDefaults
{
    WINDOW_TYPE     NO_STDIO
    EXEC_STRING     /usr/dt/bin/dtaction -user root \
                    EditAppDefaults %Arg_1"File:"%
}
ACTION EditAppDefaults
{
    WINDOW_TYPE     TERMINAL
    EXEC_STRING     /bin/sh -c 'chmod +w %Arg_1%; \
                    vi %Arg_1%; chmod -w %Arg_1%'
}
```

Creating Localized Actions

The search path for data types includes language-dependent locations. The desktop uses the value of LANG to determine the locations searched for data type definitions.

Locations for Localized Actions

Localized action definitions must be placed in the proper language-dependent directories along the actions search path.

The default search path is:

- Personal actions: *HomeDirectory*/.dt/types
- System-wide actions: /etc/dt/appconfig/types/*language*
- Built-in actions: /usr/dt/appconfig/types/*language*

▼ To Localize an Existing Action

1. Create a file in the appropriate language-dependent directory (for example, in /etc/dt/appconfig/types/japanese).

2. Copy the action definition to the language-dependent configuration file.

   For example, you might copy an action definition from

   app_root/dt/appconfig/types/C/*file*.dt

   to

   app_root/dt/appconfig/types/japanese/*newfile*.dt

3. Add a LABEL field or modify the existing LABEL field.

   ```
   LABEL    string
   ```

   Application Manager and File Manager use the label string to identify the action's icon.

4. Localize any of the following fields in the action definition:
   - For localized icons: ICON
   - For localized On Item help: DESCRIPTION
   - For localized prompts: any quoted text in the EXEC_STRING

Creating Actions for ToolTalk Applications

Note – The following information applies only to applications that support ToolTalk messaging.

Use the action type TT_MSG to create an action that sends a ToolTalk message.

```
ACTION action_name
{
    TYPE    TT_MSG
    ...
}
```

addressing and disposition Fields

- The ToolTalk addressing field is always set to TT_PROCEDURE.
- The ToolTalk disposition field defaults to the specification in the static message pattern.

Unsupported Messages

The following are not supported by TT_MSG-type actions:

- ToolTalk object-oriented messages
- Context arguments in messages

Keywords for TT_MSG Actions

Keyword	Use
TT_CLASS	Defines the value of the ToolTalk `class` message field
TT_SCOPE	Defines the value of the ToolTalk `scope` message field
TT_OPERATION	Defines the value of the ToolTalk `operation` message field.
TT_FILE	Defines the value of the ToolTalk `file` message field
TT_ARGn_MODE	Defines the value of the ToolTalk `mode` attribute for the *n*th message argument
TT_ARGn_VTYPE	Defines the value of the ToolTalk `vtype` attribute of the *n*th message argument
TT_ARGn_VALUE	Defines the value of the *n*th message argument

Creating Data Types Manually 11

There are two ways to create a data type definition:

- Using the Create Action tool. Using Create Action is covered in Chapter 9, "Creating Actions and Data Types Using Create Action."
- By manually creating the data type definition.

Creating a data type manually requires you to edit a database file.

This chapter describes how to manually create data type definitions.

See Also

- For an introduction to data types, see Chapter 8, "Introduction to Actions and Data Types."
- For reference information about data type definitions, see the `dtddsfile(4)` man page.

Reasons You Must Create a Data Type Manually

Manually creating a data type lets you use all the capabilities built into the syntax of data type definitions.

You must create an data type manually if you want to use these features of data types:

- Location (path)-based data typing
- The ability to specify actions associated with the data type other than Open and Print
- Multiple name, pattern, or content criteria for the same data type—for example, a data type based on files named `*.abc` or `*.def`
- Link-based data typing

Components of a Data Type Definition: Criteria and Attributes

A data type definition consists of two separate database definitions:

- The `DATA_ATTRIBUTES` definition.

  The `DATA_ATTRIBUTES` definition describes the data type's name and the appearance and behavior of files of this type.

- The `DATA_CRITERIA` definition.

  The `DATA_CRITERIA` definition describes the typing criteria. Each criteria definition specifies the `DATA_ATTRIBUTES` definition to which the criteria apply.

There must be at least one `DATA_CRITERIA` definition for each `DATA_ATTRIBUTES` definition; a `DATA_ATTRIBUTES` definition can have multiple `DATA_CRITERIA` associated with it.

For example, you could create an attributes definition for PostScript files that described how PostScript files look and behave in File Manager. Then, you could create two separate criteria for the PostScript data type— one based on file name and the other based on file content.

For more information, see "Defining the Data Criteria for a Data Type" on page 193.

Creating a Data Type Manually: General Steps

This section describes how to create a data type configuration file.

Configuration Files for Data Types

The requirements for configuration files containing data type definitions are:

- The files must use the naming convention *name*`.dt`
- The files must be located on the database search path. The default search path is:

Personal data types	*HomeDirectory*`/.dt/types`
System-wide data types	`/etc/dt/appconfig/types/`*language*
Built-in data types	`/usr/dt/appconfig/types/`*language*. You should not use this directory.

For information on modifying the database search path, see "Setting the Value of a Search Path" on page 115.

▼ To Create a Data Type Definition

1. Open an existing database file or create a new one.

   For more information, see the previous section, "Configuration Files for Data Types."

2. Define the data attributes for the data type using the syntax:

```
DATA_ATTRIBUTES data_type_name
{
 ICON          image_name
 DESCRIPTION   string
 attribute_field
 attribute_field
 ...
}
```

   where:

   data_type_name   A unique name given to this data type.

image_name	File name or path of an icon file. Use the base name for the file. For example, for icon files `myimage.m.pm` and `myimage.t.pm`, use `myimage`.
attribute_field	Field that defines the appearance or behavior of the data type.
string	Character string. The contents will be the on-item help for the data type.

See "Example of Creating a Personal Action and Data Type" on page 189.

3. Define the data criteria for the data type using the syntax:

```
DATA_CRITERIA criteria_name
{
  DATA_ATTRIBUTES_NAME    data_type_name
  criteria_field
  criteria_field
  ...
}
```

where:

criteria_name	Unique name for this criteria definition
data_type_name	Name used in the `DATA_ATTRIBUTES` definition
criteria_field	Field used to define the criteria for assigning a file to this data type

See "Defining the Data Criteria for a Data Type" on page 193.

4. Save the database file.
5. Create the icons for the data type.

   For more information, see "Specifying the Icon Image Used for a Data Type" on page 190.
6. If necessary, create the actions listed in the `ACTIONS` field of the attributes definition.
7. Double-click Reload Actions in the Desktop_Tools application group to reload the database.

Example of Creating a Personal Action and Data Type

Suppose your system contains an application named `xgif`, which displays GIF pictures. Ordinarily, you run the program by executing:

`xgif` *filename*

You want to be able to display GIF pictures several ways:

- By double-clicking a GIF data file
- By selecting the data file and choosing the application from the Selected menu

1. Open a new file *HomeDirectory*`/.dt/types/GifViewer.dt` for editing.
2. Type the data type definitions:

```
DATA_ATTRIBUTES Gif
{
 DESCRIPTION            Gif image file.
 ICON                   GifIcon
 ACTIONS                View
}
DATA_CRITERIA Gif_Criteria
{
 DATA_ATTRIBUTES_NAME   Gif
 NAME_PATTERN           *.gif
}
```

3. Type the action definition for the GifViewer action:

```
ACTION GifViewer
{
 EXEC_STRING        xgif %(File)Arg_1"Gif file to view:"
 WINDOW_TYPE        NO_STDIO
 DESCRIPTION        Double-click or drop a file to \
                    start the Gif viewer.
}
```

   Since the definition does not include an `ICON` field, the action will use the system's default icon.

4. Type the following map action to connect the GifViewer action to the View action listed in the data type definition. Use the `ARG_TYPE` field to restrict this view action to Gif-type files.

```
ACTION View
{
 ARG_TYPE        Gif
 TYPE            MAP
 MAP_ACTION      GifViewer
}
```

5. Save the file.
6. Double-click Reload Actions in the Desktop_Tools application group to reread the database.

Defining the Data Attributes of a Data Type

The DATA_ATTRIBUTES definition defines the appearance and behavior of the data type. It specifies the name of the data type, and provides the ability to specify:

- The File Manager icon (ICON field)
- The double-click behavior and contents of the Selected menu (ACTIONS field)
- The data type's on-item help (DESCRIPTION field)

Specifying the Icon Image Used for a Data Type

Use the ICON field to specify the icon used in File Manager. If you do not specify an icon image, File Manager displays only a label.

The value of the ICON field can be:

- A base file name.

  The base file name is the name of the file containing the icon image, minus the file-name suffixes for size (m and t) and image type (bm and pm). For example, if files are named GameIcon.m.pm and GameIcon.t.pm, use GameIcon.

  If you use the base file name, the icon files must be placed in a directory on the icon search path:
  - Personal icons: *HomeDirectory*/.dt/icons
  - System-wide icons: /etc/dt/appconfig/icons/*language*
- An absolute path to the icon file, including the full file name.

You should use the absolute path only if the icon file is not located on the icon search path. For example, if icon file GameIcon.m.pm is placed in the directory /doc/projects, which is not on the icon search path, the value of the ICON field would be /doc/projects/GameIcon.m.pm.

Table 11-1 lists icon sizes you should create and the corresponding file names.

Table 11-1 Icon Names and Sizes for Data Type Icons

Size in Pixels	Bitmap Name	Pixmap Name
32 by 32	*name*.m.bm	*name*.m.pm
16 by 16	*name*.t.bm	*name*.t.pm

Associating Data Types with Actions

There are two ways that data types are associated with actions:

- The ACTIONS field in the DATA_ATTRIBUTES definition lists the actions that will appear in File Manager's Selected menu. The first action in the list is the default (double-click) action.
- Actions can be restricted to specified data types using the action definition's ARG_TYPE field.

For example, the following data type definition creates a data type for special "readme" files created by your system administrator that use the naming convention *.rm.

```
DATA_ATTRIBUTES SysReadmeFile
{
    ICON                    SysReadMe
    ACTIONS                 Open,Respond
}
DATA_CRITERIA SysReadmeFileCriteria
{
    NAME_PATTERN            *.rm
    DATA_ATTRIBUTES_NAME    SysReadmeFile
}
```

A special Respond action is defined below for the file. It opens a writable copy of the file in Text Editor. When the file is saved and Text Editor is exited, the file is mailed to the system administrator (mail address sysadmin@utd).

```
ACTION Respond
{
    ARG_TYPE      SysReadmeFile
    EXEC_STRING   /bin/sh -c 'cp %Arg_1% $HOME/readme.temp;\
                  chmod +w $HOME/readme.temp;            \
                  dtpad $HOME/readme.temp;               \
                  cat $HOME/readme.temp |                \
                  /usr/bin/mailx sysadmin@utd;           \
                  rm $HOME/readme.temp'
    WINDOW_TYPE   NO_STDIO
}
```

Hiding Files Based on Data Type

If a file is an invisible data type, it never appears in File Manager.

Use the PROPERTIES field in the DATA_ATTRIBUTES definition to specify that objects of this type be hidden:

```
PROPERTIES     invisible
```

Specifying Behaviors When the File Is Manipulated

The following DATA_ATTRIBUTES fields are used primarily by application programmers. They specify how files behave when the user performs various desktop activities.

For more information, see the *Common Desktop Environment Programmer's Guide*, which is part of the developer environment documentation.

Field	Description
MOVE_TO_ACTION	For containers such as directories. Specifies an action to be run when a file is moved to a container of this data type.
COPY_TO_ACTION	For containers such as directories. Specifies an action to be run when a file is copied to a container of this data type.
LINK_TO_ACTION	Specifies an action to be run when a file is linked to a file of this data type.
IS_TEXT	Specifies that files of this data type contain text that can be displayed in a text box.

MEDIA	Specifies the corresponding ToolTalk media type.
MIME_TYPE	Specifies the corresponding MIME type.
X400_TYPE	Specifies the corresponding X400 type.

Defining the Data Criteria for a Data Type

The DATA_CRITERIA definition defines the criteria used to assign an object type to a file or directory.

You can use the following criteria for object typing:

Criteria	Description
File name	The file name must match a specified pattern. Use the NAME_PATTERN field.
File location	The path must match a specified pattern. Use the PATH_PATTERN field.
File contents	A specified portion of the file's contents must match specified data. Use the CONTENT field.
File mode	The file must possess the specified permissions (read, write, execute, directory). Use the MODE field.
Symbolic links	The typing is based on the file to which the object is linked.

You can use more than one criteria for a data type. However, you should not use the NAME_PATTERN and PATH_PATTERN criteria in the same data type.

Name-Based Data Types

Use the NAME_PATTERN field to specify the naming requirement. The field value can include the following wildcards:

?	Matches any single character
*	Matches any sequence of characters (including a null string)
[*cc*...]	Matches any of the characters (*c*) enclosed in brackets
[*c–c*]	Matches any of the characters in the range *c* through *c*

Examples

- The following data type definition creates a data type based on the file name. The file name must begin with QS and end with .doc.

```
DATA_ATTRIBUTES QS_Doc
{
 DESCRIPTION    This file contains a document for the QS project.
 ICON           Word_Doc
 ACTIONS        Open
}

DATA_CRITERIA QS_Doc_Criteria
{
 NAME_PATTERN   QS*.doc
 DATA_ATTRIBUTES_NAME QS_Doc
}
```

- The following definition creates a data type for directories named Demo_*n* where *n* is 0 through 9.

```
DATA_ATTRIBUTES Demo_directory
{
 DESCRIPTION    This is a directory. Double-click to open it.
 ICON           Demo
 ACTIONS        OpenInPlace,OpenNewView
}

DATA_CRITERIA Demo_directory_criteria
{
 NAME_PATTERN           Demo_[0-9]
 MODE                   d
 DATA_ATTRIBUTES_NAME   Demo_directory
}
```

Location-Based Data Types

Use the PATH_PATTERN field to specify the path. You can use the same wildcard characters as with NAME_PATTERN.

For example, the following data type uses a criteria based on path.

```
DATA_ATTRIBUTES Project_Graphics
{
   DESCRIPTIONGraphics file for the QS project. Double-click the \
              icon to see the graphic.
   ICON       QSgraphics
```

```
}
DATA_CRITERIA Project_Graphics_Criteria
{
    DATA_ATTRIBUTES_NAME    Project_Graphics
    PATH_PATTERN            */projects/QS/graphics/*
}
```

Data Types Based on Name and Location

To create a data type based on both file name and location, include the name in the PATH_PATTERN value. You cannot use both NAME_PATTERN and PATH_PATTERN in the same criteria definition.

Examples

- The QS_Source_Files data type defined below applies to all files named app*n*.c, where *n*= 1 through 9, located in subdirectories of */projects/QS.

```
DATA_ATTRIBUTES QS_Source_Files
{
    ...
}
DATA_CRITERIA QS_Source_Files_Criteria
{
 PATH_PATTERN           */projects/QS/*/app[1-9].c
 DATA_ATTRIBUTES_NAME   QS_Source_Files
}
```

- The following data type applies to all files in the directory /doc/project1 named ch*nn*.*xxx* where *n* is 0 through 9, and *xxx* is any three-character filename suffix.

```
DATA_ATTRIBUTES ChapterFiles
{
 DESCRIPTION        Chapter file for the project document.
 ICON               chapter
 ACTIONS            Edit,Print
}

DATA_CRITERIA Chapter_Criteria
{
 PATH_PATTERN           /doc/project1/ch[0-9][0-9].???
 DATA_ATTRIBUTES_NAME   ChapterFiles
}
```

Using File Modes as a Typing Criteria

Use the MODE field to specify the required permissions.

Mode criteria are usually used in combination with name-based, location-based, or content-based data typing. They allow you to limit a data type to a file or directory, or to specify the required read, write, and execute permissions.

The MODE field can include the following logical operators and characters:

Operator	Description
!	Logical operator NOT
&	Logical operator AND
|	Logical OR

Character	Description
f	The data type applies only to files
d	The data type applies only to directories
r	The file is readable by any user
w	The file is writable by any user
x	The file is executable by any user
l	The file is a link

The default for a particular mode is that the mode does not matter.

Examples

- The following mode fields restrict the data type as described:

f&!w	Read-only files
!w	Read-only files and directories
f&x	Executable files
f&r&x	Files that are both writable and executable
x|!w	Files that are executable or read-only

- The following data type definition creates an data type for read-only, non-executable files whose file names follow the naming convention `*.doc`. It assumes that a View action has been defined for the data type.

```
DATA_ATTRIBUTES ReadOnlyDocument
{
 ICON           read_only
 DESCRIPTION    This document is not writable. Double-clicking \
                runs your editor with a read-only copy of the   \
                file.
 ACTIONS        View
}

DATA_CRITERIA ReadOnlyDocument_Criteria
{
 NAME_PATTERN          *.doc
 MODE                  !d&!x&!w
 DATA_ATTRIBUTES_NAME  ReadOnlyDocument
}
```

Content-Based Data Typing

Use the `CONTENT` field to specify data typing based on the content of the file. Content-based data typing can be used in combination with name- or location-based data typing.

The typing can be based on either string or numeric content for files. The first byte in the file is numbered 0.

- For string content of a file, use the syntax:

  `CONTENT` *starting_byte* `string` *string*

- For number content of a file, use the syntax:

  `CONTENT` *starting_byte* `byte` *number*
  `CONTENT` *starting_byte* `short` *number*
  `CONTENT` *starting_byte* `long` *number*

- For the contents of a directory, use the syntax:

  `CONTENT 0 filename "`*file_name*`"`

  Use standard C notation for octal (leading `o`) and hexidecimal (leading `oX`) numbers.

Note – Use of content-based data typing will result in slower system performance. Wherever possible, use name- and location-based typing instead.

For example, the following data type, Writable_Wingz, applies to all files with write permission containing the string WNGZ at the beginning of the file.

```
DATA_ATTRIBUTES Writable_Wingz
{
 ...
}

DATA_CRITERIA Writable_Wingz_Criteria
{
 CONTENT               0 string WNGZ
 MODE                  w&!d
 DATA_ATTRIBUTES_NAME  Writable_Wingz
}
```

▼ To Create a Data Type with Several Independent Criteria

You can create a data type with several independent criteria—that is, the file is assigned to the data type if it meets *either* (or both) of the criteria.

1. Create the DATA_ATTRIBUTES definition for the data type.
2. Create a DATA_CRITERIA definition for each criteria.

   Use the DATA_ATTRIBUTES_NAME field to connect each criteria to the same DATA_ATTRIBUTES definition.

For example, the following definitions create the Mif data type. Typing is based on name or content.

```
DATA_ATTRIBUTES Mif
{
    ICON                  Frame
    ACTION_LIST           Open,Print
}

DATA_CRITERIA Mif_Name_Criteria
{
    DATA_ATTRIBUTES_NAME      Mif
    NAME_PATTERN              *.mif
}
```

```
DATA_CRITERIA Mif_Content_Criteria
{
    DATA_ATTRIBUTES_NAME        Mif
    CONTENT                     1 string MIFFile
}
```

Creating Localized Data Types

The search path for data types includes language-dependent locations. The desktop uses the value of LANG to determine the locations searched for data type definitions.

Locations for Localized Data Types

Localized data type definitions must be placed in the proper language-dependent directories along the actions search path.

The default search path is:

- Personal actions: *HomeDirectory*`/.dt/types`
- System-wide actions: `/etc/dt/appconfig/types/`*language*
- Built-in actions: `/usr/dt/appconfig/types/`*language*

▼ To Localize a Data Type

1. Create a file in the appropriate language-dependent directory (for example, in `/etc/dt/appconfig/types/japanese`).
2. Copy the data type definition to the language-dependent configuration file.
3. Localize one or more fields in the data type definition.

Creating Icons for the Desktop 12

Desktop icons are associated with:

- Action files and data types in File Manager and Application Manager
- Front Panel controls
- Minimized application windows
- Graphics used by applications such as palettes and toolbars
- Workspace backdrop

Note – The development environment documentation contains additional information about desktop icons. See Chapter 4, "Visual Design," in the *Style Guide and Certification Checklist*.

Icon Image Files

For the desktop to use an icon image, the icon image file must:

- Be in the proper format.
- Use the proper file-naming conventions.
- Use the desktop size conventions.

- Be located in a directory along the icon search path.
- Be called by the desktop construct using the proper syntax. For example, if you create a new control for the Front Panel, use the ICON field in the Front Panel definition to specify the icon image to use for the control.

Icon File Formats

For a color display, use X pixmap (XPM) format icon files, which typically have a .pm suffix. Otherwise, use X bitmap (XBM) format files, which typically have a .bm suffix. If transparency is used in the pixmap file, a mask file (_m.bm) is generated when the .bm file is created. See "Icon Search Path" on page 122 for more information about how the desktop finds these files.

Icon File Names

Each icon and backdrop image is stored as a separate file. Typically, an icon is specified with the base part of its file name. For example, an icon might be referenced with the name `mail` when the file is actually stored as:

`/usr/dt/appconfig/icons/`*`language`*`/mail.l.pm`

The file-naming convention of adding suffixes helps group icons by size and type. Icon names for desktop components are in these general formats:

basename.size.format

Or

basename.format

where:

basename	The image base name used to reference the image
size	A letter indicating the size: l (large) m (medium) s (small) t (tiny)
format	File format: pm (pixmap) bm (bitmap)

Icon Size Conventions

Table 12-1 shows the recommended pixel dimensions for desktop icons.

Table 12-1 Icon Sizes and File Names

Icon Size	Bitmap Name	Pixmap Name
16 by 16 (tiny)	*name*.t.bm	*name*.t.pm
24 by 24 (small)	*name*.s.bm	*name*.s.pm
32 by 32 (medium)	*name*.m.bm	*name*.m.pm
48 by 48 (large)	*name*.l.bm	*name*.l.pm

Table 12-2 shows the icon sizes used by the desktop components. In some cases, the size of the icon used depends on the display resolution.

Table 12-2 Desktop Components and Their Icon Sizes

Desktop Component	High Resolution	Medium Resolution	Low Resolution
File Manager and Application Manager (View by Name and Icon)	medium	medium	medium
File Manager and Application Manager (View by Name and Small Icon)	tiny	tiny	tiny
Main Front Panel controls	large	large	medium
Front Panel subpanels	medium	medium	tiny
Front Panel switch controls	small	small	tiny
Minimized windows	large	large	medium

For example, if you specify an icon named `mail` for a data type, have a color display, and have set the File Manager preferences to small icons, the icon image used is `mail.t.pm`.

Icon Search Path

The desktop finds an icon file, or image, by searching for the file in a list of directories. This list of directories, called the *icon search path,* is determined by the value of several environment variables. Which variables are used and how they are put together to create the icon search path are discussed in "Icon Search Path" on page 122.

The default search path is:

- Built-in icons: `/usr/dt/appconfig/icons/`*language*
- System-wide icons: `/etc/dt/appconfig/icons/`*language*
- Personal icons: *HomeDirectory*`/.dt/icons`

Accessing Icons across the Network

The desktop can access icons on remote systems. For information on creating an icon server, see "Configuring Database, Icon, and Help Services" on page 101.

Icon Associations

To enable quicker object recognition, you can associate icons with:

- Actions and data types
- Controls in the Front Panel and subpanels
- Minimized application windows

Specifying Icon Files

For icons used for actions, data types, and in the Front Panel or subpanels, specify only the base name of the icon (no suffixes). The correct suffixes are added automatically based on your display resolution, color support, and File Manager view options (such as By Small Icons).

To override the search path, provide the complete path and name of the icon.

▼ To Associate an Icon with an Action or Data Type

1. Specify the icon using the `ICON` field.

   If you follow the appropriate naming conventions for icon files, specify only the base name of the icon. The correct icon will be displayed based on the resolution and color support of your display.

2. Create the following icon sizes:
   - Actions: large, medium, and tiny
   - Data types: medium and tiny

Example of an Action Definition

The following example is an action definition for starting the Island Paint™ drawing tool. The icons `Ipaint.l` and `Ipaint.s` are associated with the action.

```
ACTION              IslandPaintOpenDoc
{
    WINDOW_TYPE     NO-STDIO
    ICON            Ipaint
    EXEC_STRING      /usr/bin/IslandPaint %Arg_1"File to open:"%
}
```

If you are using color icons, the desktop first appends `.pm` when looking for the actual icon files. Otherwise (or if no match is found with `.pm`), the desktop appends `.bm`.

Example of Data Type Definition

The following data type definition associates the icons `comprsd.l` and `comprsd.s` with compressed files:

```
DATA_ATTRIBUTES      COMPRESSED
{

    ICON            comprsd
    ACTIONS         Uncompress
    DESCRIPTION     A COMPRESSED file has been compressed by the \
                    'compress' command to take up less space.

}
```

▼ To Display an Icon in a Front Panel Control

1. Specify the image name using the `ICON` field.

   If the control monitors a file (`MONITOR_TYPE` is set to mail or file), use the `ALTERNATE_ICON` field to specify the icons used when the change is detected.

   You can also provide animation for buttons and drop zone controls.

2. Create the following icon sizes:
   - Main Panel and subpanels: large, medium, and tiny
   - Workspace switch: small

Example

The following control changes appearance when a file named `report` is placed in the `/doc/ftp/pub/` directory. When the file is not there, the `NoReport.pm` icon is displayed; when the file is there, `Report.pm` is displayed.

```
CONTROL MonitorReport
{
    CONTAINER_NAME container_name
    TYPE           ICON
    MONITOR_TYPE   file
    FILE_NAME      /doc/ftp/pub/report
    ICON           NoReport
    ALTERNATE_ICON Report
}
```

▼ To Associate an Icon with an Application Window

1. Set the `iconImage` resource for Workspace Manager as follows:

   `Dtwm*`*clientname*`*iconImage:` *icon_file_name*

   To determine the correct value for *clientname*, open Application Manager and double-click Window Properties in the Desktop_Tools application group. When you select a window, its properties are listed. The WM_CLASS property displays the window's class name in quotes.

   For more information about setting resources, see "Setting Application Resources" on page 256.

2. Choose Restart Workspace Manager from the Workspace menu.

To verify that the icon has been recognized by Workspace Manager, minimize the window whose icon you are trying to modify.

Note – Some applications do not allow their default window icon to be overridden.

▼ To Use File Manager as an Icon Browser

1. Copy the file `/usr/dt/examples/`*language*`/IconBrowse.dt` to the *HomeDirectory*`/.dt/types/Iconbrowse.dt` directory.

2. Open Application Manager and double-click Reload Actions in the Desktop_Tools application group.

When you change to a directory that contains icons (`.bm` and `.pm` files), each icon is displayed next to its name. For example, if you change to the `/usr/dt/appconfig/icons/`*language* directory, you will see many of the desktop icons.

Note – Enabling icon browsing on low-memory systems may cause File Manager to display directories more slowly.

Images larger than 256 x 256 are not displayed in the default configuration.

To disable icon browsing:

1. Remove your personal copy of the `IconBrowse.dt` file.

2. Open Application Manager and double-click Reload Actions in the Desktop_Tools application group.

Icon Design Recommendations

Use a common theme among related icons. For example, if you are designing icons for an application, have purposeful similarities between the application's icon and icons for data files.

Be sure the two-color version of any color icon you design is acceptable. If the icon is displayed on a monochrome or grayscale display (or if there are not enough colors available), the icon is automatically displayed in its two-color form.

To conserve system color usage, try to limit icon color use to those provided by the desktop.(Icons created using Icon Editor will be use only desktop colors.)

For the sizes used by the desktop components, see Table 12-1, "Icon Sizes and File Names," on page 203.

Color Usage

Desktop icons use a palette of 22 colors including:

- Eight static grays
- Eight static colors: red, blue, green, cyan, magenta, yellow, black, and white
- Six dynamic colors: foreground, background, top shadow, bottom shadow, select, and transparent

This palette creates attractive, easy-to-read icons without overtaking color resources needed by other applications. Most icons provided with the desktop use grays accented with color.

The transparent color is useful for creating icons that have the illusion of being nonrectangular because the color behind the icon shows through.

Advanced Front Panel Customization 13

Users can customize the Front Panel using its pop-up menus and the Install Icon controls in the subpanels.

This chapter covers customizing the Front Panel by creating and editing configuration files.

See Also

- For reference information on Front Panel controls and configuration, see the `dtfpfile(4X)` man page.
- For reference information about the Workspace Manager, see the `dtwm(1)` and `dtwmrc(4)` man pages.

Front Panel Configuration Files

The Front Panel is defined in a database of configuration files.

The configuration files provide a way to customize the Front Panel. Certain modifications can only be done by editing a configuration file, including:

- Adding a new control position to the Main Panel.
- Adding special types of controls, such as client windows.
- Changing certain default behaviors—for example, whether the Front Panel controls respond to a single- or double-click.

To provide maximum flexibility in configuring the panel, these files can be personal, system-wide, or located on other systems.

The Front Panel is created and managed by the Workspace Manager.

Default Front Panel Configuration File

The default Front Panel is defined in the Front Panel configuration file `/usr/dt/appconfig/types/`*language*`/dtwm.fp`.

This file should not be altered.

Search Path for Front Panel Configuration Files

The Front Panel definition can be distributed among any number of files located locally or on remote systems.

Files used to define the Front Panel must meet these requirements:

- The file name must end in `.fp`; for example, `mail.fp`.
- The file must be located along the actions database search path.

The default actions database search path includes these directories, searched in the following order:

HomeDirectory`/.dt/types`	Personal customizations
`/etc/dt/appconfig/types/`*language*	System-wide customizations
`/usr/dt/appconfig/types/`*language*	Built-in panel and controls

An additional directory, *HomeDirectory*/.dt/types/fp_dynamic, is used for personal customizations made with the user interface. Do not use this directory for manual customizations.

The actions database search path may include additional directories added to configure the system for networking. In particular, additional remote locations are added when the system is configured to access an application server. For more information, see "Database (Action/Data Types) Search Path" on page 120.

How the Front Panel Is Assembled: Precedence Rules

The Front Panel is assembled from all the configuration files located on the actions database search path.

Where there is a conflict between components of the definition, precedence rules determine which definition is used. Two components are in conflict with one another when they:

- Have the same control name, CONTAINER_NAME, and CONTAINER_TYPE.
- Or, they compete for the same position (by having different names but the same CONTAINER_NAME, CONTAINER_TYPE, and POSITION_HINTS).

The Front Panel uses these precedence rules:

- If components have the same control name and container name and type, the component read first is used.

  For example, if both a system-wide and built-in control contain these fields but are otherwise different:

  ```
  CONTROL TextEditor
  {
   CONTAINER_TYPE BOX
   CONTAINER_NAME Top
   ...
  }
  ```

  then the system-wide control has precedence.

- If two components complete for the same position, they are placed in the order in which they are read.

For example, if a user creates a new personal control for the Main Panel (`CONTAINER_TYPE` BOX and `CONTAINER_NAME` Top) and assigns it `POSITION_HINTS` 5, the personal control will bump the built-in control and all other controls with higher position numbers one position to the right.

Note – When you are modifying a control by creating a new system-wide or personal version of it, the new control definition must specify the same control name, `CONTAINER_NAME`, and `CONTAINER_TYPE`. Otherwise, the new control will appear in addition to the existing control.

Dynamically Created Front Panel Files

When the user customizes the Front Panel using the Install Icon control and pop-up menus, files are written to the directory *HomeDirectory*`/.dt/types/fp_dynamic`.

The Front Panel creates an additional file, *HomeDirectory*`/.dt/sessions/dtwmfp.session`, that is used to save and restore the state of the customized Front Panel for each session.

Administering User Interface Customizations

Users can use the controls' pop-up menus and Install Icon controls to extensively customize the Front Panel.

This section describes how to:

- Prevent certain personal customizations. For example, you may want to make it impossible for a user to delete a control.
- Undo personal customizations. For example, a user might request that you restore a single control accidentally deleted.

▼ To Prevent Personal Customizations

1. If the control is a built-in control, copy its definition from `/usr/dt/appconfig/types/`*language*`/dtwm.fp` to `/etc/dt/appconfig/types/`*language*`/`*name*`.fp`.

2. Add the following line to the control definition:

```
LOCKED    True
```

▼ To Restore a Deleted Control or Subpanel

The Restore Front Panel action in the Desktop_Tools application group removes all Front Panel customizations made with the user interface. Users can use this action to remove all their personal customizations made with the Front Panel's pop-up menus.

Use the following procedure to restore an individual control.

♦ In the *HomeDirectory*/.dt/types/fp_dynamic directory, remove the file that was created when the user deleted the control. The control will have the same name as the original control that was deleted.

  For example, if the user deleted the Icon Editor control, a file in the fp_dynamic directory will contain:

```
CONTROL IconEditor
{
   ...
    DELETE    True
}
```

When the user deletes a subpanel, a separate dynamic file is created for the subpanel and for each control in the subpanel.

Organization of the Front Panel Definition

The Front Panel is built by assembling definitions for its components. Each of these components has required syntax that defines where the component is placed in the Front Panel, what the component looks like, and how it behaves.

Front Panel Components

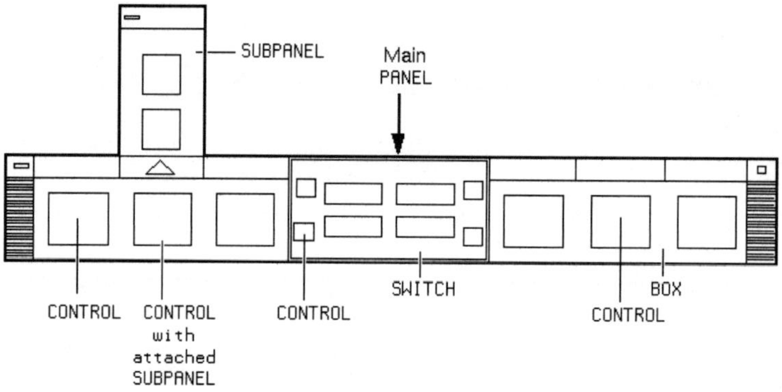

Figure 13-1 Front Panel components

The Front Panel is assembled from the outside in:

- The PANEL is the top-level container, or parent, for the entire Front Panel.
- The PANEL is a container for one or more BOXes.
- A BOX is a container for one or more CONTROLs.

There are two special types of containers:

- A SUBPANEL is associated with a particular control (the control is the container for the subpanel). Subpanels "slide up" from the control with which they are associated.
- The SWITCH contains the buttons for changing workspaces plus additional controls.

General Syntax of the Front Panel Definition

Each component in the Front Panel is defined separately using the syntax:

```
COMPONENT  name
{
  KEYWORD        value
  KEYWORD        value
  ...
}
```

Some keywords are required, others are optional. For more information, see the `dtfpfile(4X)` man page.

PANEL Definition

The PANEL is the top-level component. Its definition includes:

- The Front Panel name
- Fields describing the general appearance and behavior of the entire Front Panel

```
PANEL front_panel_name
{
    KEYWORD          value
    KEYWORD          value
    ...
```

The *front_panel_name* is a unique name for the Front Panel. The default name is "FrontPanel."

BOX Definitions

A BOX definition describes:

- The BOX name
- Which PANEL the box is in (CONTAINER_NAME)
- The position of the box in the PANEL (POSITION_HINTS)
- Fields describing appearance and behavior that apply to the entire box

```
BOX box_name
{
    CONTAINER_NAME      front_panel_name
    POSITION_HINTS      position
    KEYWORD             value
    KEYWORD             value
    ...
}
```

CONTROL Definitions

A CONTROL definition describes:

- The CONTROL name
- Whether the control is in a box, subpanel, or switch (CONTAINER_TYPE)
- Which box, subpanel, or switch the control is in (CONTAINER_NAME)
- The position of the CONTROL in the BOX (POSITION_HINTS).
- Fields describing appearance and behavior of the control

```
CONTROL control_name
{
    CONTAINER_TYPE      BOX or SUBPANEL or SWITCH
    CONTAINER_NAME      box_name or subpanel_name or switch_name
    TYPE                control_type
    POSITION_HINTS      position
    KEYWORD             value
    KEYWORD             value
    ...
}
```

SUBPANEL Definitions

A SUBPANEL definition describes:

- The SUBPANEL name
- The name of the control to which the subpanel is attached (CONTAINER_NAME)
- Fields describing appearance and behavior specific to the subpanel

```
SUBPANEL subpanel_name
{
    CONTAINER_NAME      control_name
    KEYWORD             value
    KEYWORD             value
   ...
}
```

SWITCH Definition

The SWITCH definition describes:

- The SWITCH name
- Which BOX the SWITCH is in (CONTAINER_NAME)
- The position of the SWITCH within the BOX (POSITION_HINTS)
- Fields describing the appearance and behavior of the SWITCH

```
SWITCH switch_name
{
    CONTAINER_NAME      box_name
    POSITION_HINTS      position
    KEYWORD             value
    KEYWORD             value
   ...
}
```

Modifying the Main Panel

The Main Panel is the Front Panel window, excluding the subpanels.

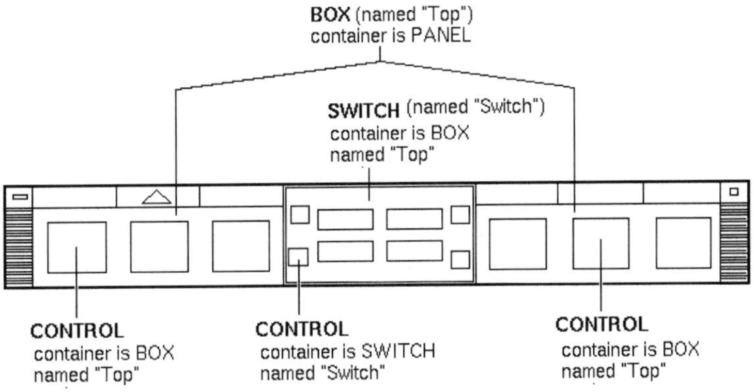

Figure 13-2 Main Panel containers

Modifications you can make include:

- Adding or removing controls
- Interchanging the positions of controls

▼ To Add a Control to the Main Panel

1. Create a Front Panel configuration file:
   - System-wide: `/etc/dt/appconfig/types/`*language*`/*.fp`
   - Personal: *HomeDirectory*`/.dt/types/*.fp`

2. Define the control in the file.

   Use the `CONTAINER_NAME` and `CONTAINER_TYPE` fields to specify the container for the control:

   ```
   CONTAINER_NAME   Top
   CONTAINER_TYPE   BOX
   ```

   Use `POSITION_HINTS` to specify the left-to-right placement of the control. Since customizations have precedence over built-in controls, the new control will "bump" the existing control with that position one position to the right.

3. Save the configuration file.

4. Create an icon for the Front Panel control.

   See "Specifying the Icon Used by a Control" on page 223.

5. Choose Restart Workspace Manager from the Workspace menu.

For example, the following control definition placed in the file `/etc/dt/appconfig/types/`*language*`/audio.fp` inserts an audio application control between the Clock and Calendar controls.

```
CONTROL AudioApplication
{
 TYPE              icon
 CONTAINER_NAME    Top
 CONTAINER_TYPE    BOX
 ICON              AudioApp
 POSITION_HINTS    2
 PUSH_ACTION       StartAudioApplication
 PUSH_RECALL       true
}
```

▼ To Remove a Control

1. Create a Front Panel configuration file:
   - System-wide: `/etc/dt/appconfig/types/`*language*`/`*name*`.fp`
   - Personal: *HomeDirectory*`/.dt/types/`*name*`.fp`

2. Copy the definition of the control you want to delete to the new file.

   If the control is built-in, its definition is in `/usr/dt/appconfig/types/`*language*`/dtwm.fp`.

   You do not need to copy the entire definition. However, the portion you copy must include the fields `CONTAINER_NAME` and `CONTAINER_TYPE`.

3. Add the `DELETE` field to the definition:

   ```
   DELETE   True
   ```

4. Save the configuration file

5. Choose Restart Workspace Manager from the Workspace menu.

For example, the following control definition placed in the file `/etc/dt/appconfig/types/`*language*`/TrashCan.fp` removes the Trash Can control from the Front Panel.

```
CONTROL Trash
{
 CONTAINER_NAME   Top
 CONTAINER_TYPE   BOX
 DELETE           True
}
```

▼ To Modify a Control

Use this procedure when you need to modify a control definition—for example, to change its icon image.

1. Copy the entire control definition from `/usr/dt/appconfig/types/`*language*`/dtwm.fp` to:
   - System-wide: `/etc/dt/appconfig/types/`*language*`/`*name*`.fp`
   - Personal: *HomeDirectory*`/.dt/types/`*name*`.fp`.
2. Edit the field you want to change. You can also add additional fields.
3. Save the file
4. Choose Restart Workspace Manager from the Workspace menu.

▼ To Interchange the Position of Controls

1. Copy the control definitions for the controls whose positions you want to change from `/usr/dt/appconfig/types/`*language*`/dtwm.fp` to:
   - System-wide: `/etc/dt/appconfig/types/`*language*`/`*name*`.fp`
   - Personal: *HomeDirectory*`/.dt/types/`*name*`.fp`.

   You must copy the entire control definition for each control to be moved..
2. Interchange the values of the `POSITION_HINTS` fields of the control definitions.
3. Save the file
4. Choose Restart Workspace Manager from the Workspace menu.

For example, the following definitions placed in a file `/etc/dt/appconfig/types/C/MailHelp.fp` interchange the positions of the Mail and Help Manager controls and lock these controls against personal changes.

```
CONTROL Mail
{
    POSITION_HINTS      12
    LOCKED              True
    ...the rest of the control definition
}

CONTROL Help
{
    POSITION_HINTS      5
    LOCKED              True
    ...the rest of the control definition
}
```

▼ To Replace a Front Panel Control

♦ Create another control definition with the same:

- *control_name*
- CONTAINER_NAME value

For example, the following two controls are defined in two different configuration files. The controls have the same control name and container name and are therefore considered the same control.

- Definition in /etc/dt/appconfig/types/C/SysControls.fp:

```
Control ImportantApplication
{
  CONTAINER_NAME      Top
  CONTAINER_TYPE      BOX
  POSITION_HINTS      2
 ...
```

- Definition in *HomeDirectory*/.dt/types/MyControls.fp:

```
Control ImportantApplication
{
  CONTAINER_NAME      Top
  CONTAINER_TYPE      BOX
  POSITION_HINTS      6
 ...
```

The personal control has precedence, so the control will be located at position 6.

Specifying the Icon Used by a Control

The control definition's `ICON` field defines the icon image used for the control.

The value of the `ICON` field can be:

- A base file name.

  The base file name is the name of the file containing the icon image minus the file-name suffixes for size (`m` and `t`) and image type (`bm` and `pm`). For example, if files are named `MyGame.l.pm` and `MyGame.m.pm`, use `MyGame`.

  If you use the base file name, the icon files must be placed in a directory on the icon search path:
  - Personal icons: *HomeDirectory*`/.dt/icons`
  - System-wide icons: `/etc/dt/appconfig/icons/`*language*

- An absolute path to the icon file, including the full file name.

  You should use the absolute path only if the icon file is not located on the icon search path.

The size icon you need depends on the location of the control:

Location	Size
Main Panel	48 by 48 pixels (*name*`.l.pm` or *name*`.l.bm`)
Subpanel	24 by 24 pixels (*name*`.s.pm` or *name*`.s.bm`)

Place the icon file in one of these locations:

- Personal icons: *HomeDirectory*`/.dt/icons`
- System-wide icons: `/etc/dt/appconfig/icons/`*language*

Creating and Modifying Subpanels

Users can create and modify subpanels using the Front Panel pop-up menus.

This section discusses how to provide system-wide customization, which requires you to modify the Front Panel configuration files.

A subpanel is "attached" to a control in the Main Panel.

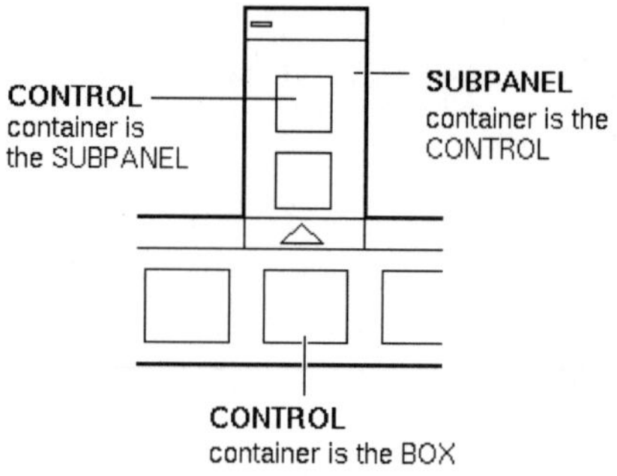

Figure 13-3 A subpanel's container is the control to which it is attached

The attachment is done in the subpanel definition. The `CONTAINER_NAME` field specifies the control to which the subpanel is attached:

```
CONTROL control_name
{
   ...
}

SUBPANEL subpanel_name
{
   CONTAINER_NAME        control_name
   ...
}
```

▼ To Create a New System-Wide Subpanel

1. Locate the *control_name* of the control in the Main Panel to which you want to attach the subpanel.

   If the control is one of the built-in controls, its definition is in `/usr/dt/appconfig/types/`*language*`/dtwm.fp`.

2. Create a new file `/etc/dt/appconfig/types/`*language*`/*.fp`.

3. Define the subpanel:

```
SUBPANEL subpanel_name
{
  CONTAINER_NAME control_name
  TITLE          value
  KEYWORD        value
  ...
}
```

4. Save the new configuration file.

5. Choose Restart Workspace Manager from the Workspace menu.

Customizing the Built-in Subpanels

You can modify general properties (such as the title) and the contents of the built-in subpanels.

▼ *To Modify General Properties of a Built-In Subpanel*

1. Create a new Front Panel configuration file:
   - System-wide: `/etc/dt/appconfig/types/`*language*`/`*name*`.fp`
   - Personal: *HomeDirectory*`/.dt/types/`*name*`.fp`.

2. Copy the entire default `SUBPANEL` definition from `/usr/dt/appconfig/types/`*language*`/dtwm.fp` to the new file:

```
SUBPANEL    subpanel_name
{
  ...
}
```

3. Modify the subpanel definition.

4. Save the new configuration file.

5. Choose Restart Workspace Manager from the Workspace menu.

For example, the following definition, placed in the file /users/janice/.dt/types/PerApps.fp, changes the name of the Personal Applications subpanel:

```
SUBPANEL PersAppsSubpanel
{
    CONTAINER_NAME     TextEditor
    TITLE              Janice's Applications
}
```

To Add a System-Wide Control to a Built-In Subpanel

1. Create a Front Panel configuration file /etc/dt/appconfig/types/*language*/*name*.fp.
2. Define the system-wide control in the file.

   Use the CONTAINER_NAME and CONTAINER_TYPE fields to specify the container for the control:

   ```
   CONTROL control_name
   {
    CONTAINER_NAME     subpanel_name
    CONTAINER_TYPE     SUBPANEL
    ...
   }
   ```

   See "Defining Front Panel Controls" on page 228.
3. Save the configuration file.
4. Choose Restart Workspace Manager from the Workspace menu.

For example, the following control defined in a new file /etc/dt/appconfig/types/*language*/DigitalClock.fp adds the DigitalClock (in the Desktop_Tools application group) to the Personal Applications subpanel for all users.

```
CONTROL DigitalClockControl
{
    TYPE           icon
    CONTAINER_NAME PerAppsSubpanel
    CONTAINER_TYPE SUBPANEL
    ICON           Dtdgclk
```

```
    PUSH_ACTION     DigitalClock
    PUSH_RECALL     True
}
```

To Remove a Control from a Built-In Subpanel

- Use the same procedure as for removing a Main Panel control. See "To Remove a Control" on page 220.

To Remove the Install Icon Control

- Add the following field to the subpanel definition:

```
CONTROL_INSTALL  False
```

To Change the Auto-Close Behavior of Subpanels

The default behavior of subpanels is to close when the user chooses a control, unless the user has moved the subpanel from its original position.

The Front Panel can be configured to keep subpanels open until the user explicitly closes them.

1. Create a new Front Panel configuration file in:
   - System-wide: `/etc/dt/appconfig/types/`*language*`/*.fp`
   - Personal: *HomeDirectory*`/.dt/types/*.fp`
2. Copy the default `PANEL` definition from `/usr/dt/appconfig/types/`*language*`/dtwm.fp` to the new file:

```
PANEL FrontPanel
{
  ...
}
```

3. Add the following field to the `PANEL` definition:

```
SUBPANEL_UNPOST     False
```

4. Save the new configuration file.
5. Choose Restart Workspace Manager from the Workspace menu.

Defining Front Panel Controls

The user can create personal controls by dropping icons on the Install Icon controls.

While this provides easy customizability, the functionality it provides is a subset of the capabilities of Front Panel controls. For example, a control created using the Install Icon control cannot:

- Provide animation
- Display a client window
- Change appearance when an event occurs (for example, upon receiving new mail)

This section describes how to manually create Front Panel controls.

For reference information on the syntax of Front Panel controls, see the `dtfpfile(4X)` man page.

Front Panel Control Definitions

The structure of a Front Panel control definition is:

```
CONTROL control_name
{
  TYPE              control_type
  CONTAINER_NAME    value
  CONTAINER_TYPE    value
  other fields defining appearance and behavior
}
```

Control Types

The `TYPE` field in the control definition specifies the basic behavior of the control.

Control TYPE	Control Behavior
`icon`	(Default). The control will run a specified action when the user clicks the control or drops a file on it.
`blank`	Placeholder used to adjust spacing of controls.

`busy`	Busy light. The control blinks (toggles images) when an action is invoked
`client`	A client window in the Front Panel.
`clock`	Clock.
`date`	Displays the current date.
`file`	Represents a file. Choosing the control runs the default action for the file.

▼ To Create a New Control

This section describes the general steps for defining a control and describes how to create various types of controls.

1. If the control will have a `PUSH_ACTION` and/or `DROP_ACTION`, create the action definitions. These are the actions that run when the user clicks the control or drops a file on it.
2. Create the icon image files for the control.

   For information about icon sizes, names, and locations, see "Icon Image Files" on page 201.
3. Create a new Front Panel configuration file in:
   - System-wide: `/etc/dt/appconfig/types/`*language*`/*.fp`
   - Personal: *HomeDirectory*`/.dt/types/*.fp`
4. Add the control definition to the file.
5. Save the file.
6. Choose Restart Workspace Manager from the Workspace menu.

Creating a Control that Runs an Action When Clicked

Use these fields to define the control's behavior:

- `TYPE`: Set to `icon`
- `PUSH_ACTION`: Specifies the name of the action to be run

For example, the following control, which will be put in the Personal Applications subpanel, runs a game the user has acquired:

```
CONTROL Ball
{
    TYPE                 icon
    CONTAINER_NAME       PersAppsSubpanel
    CONTAINER_TYPE       SUBPANEL
    ICON                 ball
    PUSH_ACTION          RunBallGame
    HELP_STRING          "Choose this control to play Ball."
}
```

The following control will be located in the upper left corner of the switch. It starts an action named CutDisp.

```
CONTROL StartCutDisp
{
  TYPE              icon
  CONTAINER_NAME    Switch
  CONTAINER_TYPE    SWITCH
  POSITION_HINTS    first
  ICON              cutdisp
  HELP_STRING       "Choose this control to run cutdisp."
  PUSH_ACTION       CutDisp
}
```

Creating a Control that Opens a File

Use these fields to define the control's behavior:

- `TYPE`: Set to `file`
- `FILE_NAME`: Specifies the path of the file to be opened
- `PUSH_ACTION`: Set to `Open`

There must be an Open action defined for the data type of the file.

For example, the following control will be located on the far right side of the Main Panel. It starts Text Editor with the data file `/users/ellen/PhoneList.txt`. The Open action for `*.txt` files is part of the default action database.

```
CONTROL EditPhoneList
{
    TYPE             file
    FILE_NAME        /users/ellen/PhoneList.txt
```

```
    CONTAINER_NAME Top
    CONTAINER_TYPE BOX
    POSITION_HINTS last
    ICON           PhoneBook
    HELP_STRING    "This control displays Ellen's phone list."
    PUSH_ACTION    Open
}
```

Creating a Control that Behaves as a Drop Zone

Use the DROP_ACTION field to specify the action that runs when the user drops a file on the control. The action must be capable of accepting a file argument.

Frequently, a control definition includes both a PUSH_ACTION and DROP_ACTION field. You can use the same action for the push and drop action.

For example, the following control, located in the Personal Applications subpanel, runs the X client xwud, which takes a file argument.

```
CONTROL Run_xwud
{
    CONTAINER_NAME     PerAppsSubpanel
    CONTAINER_TYPE     SUBPANEL
    POSITION_HINTS     2
    ICON               XwudImage
    PUSH_ACTION        RunXwud
    DROP_ACTION        RunXwud
}
```

Creating a Control that Monitors a File

Use these fields to define the control's behavior:

- TYPE: Specify one of the following values:

icon	Use this type if you want to specify a PUSH_ACTION and/or DROP_ACTION for the control.
file	Use this type if you want the control, when chosen, to behave like the file when the file's icon is double-clicked in File Manager.

- ICON and ALTERNATE_ICON: Describe the images used to indicate the non-changed and changed state of the monitored file.

- MONITOR_TYPE: Describes the conditions causing the image to change. Use one of the following values:

mail	The control will change appearance when information is added to the file.
file	The control will change when the specified file becomes non-empty.

- FILE_NAME: Specifies the file to be monitored.

For example, the following control looks for the presence of a file named meetings that you expect to be transferred to your system using anonymous ftp. The control is placed at the top of the Personal Applications subpanel.

```
CONTROL MonitorCalendar
{
    TYPE            file
    CONTAINER_NAME  PersonalApps
    CONTAINER_TYPE  SUBPANEL
    POSITION_HINTS  first
    FILE_NAME       /users/ftp/meetings
    MONITOR_TYPE    file
    ICON            meetingsno
    ALTERNATE_ICON  meetingsyes
}
```

Creating a One-Instance (Toggle) Control

A one-instance control checks to see whether the process started by the PUSH_ACTION is already running. If the process is not running, the PUSH_ACTION is run. If the process is already running, the window is moved to the top of the window stack in the current workspace.

Use these fields to define the control's behavior:

- PUSH_RECALL: Set to True.
- CLIENT_NAME: Specifies the name of the client to the control.

  The value of CLIENT_NAME must match the first string (*res_name*) in the WM_CLASS property on the application's top-level window. For more information, see the xprop(1) man page.
- PUSH_ACTION: Describes the action run when the user clicks the control.

For example, the following control runs one instance of an application whose action is named MyEditor.

```
CONTROL MyEditor
{
    TYPE            icon
    CONTAINER_NAME  Top
    CONTAINER_TYPE  BOX
    POSITION_HINTS  15
    PUSH_RECALL     True
    CLIENT_NAME     BestEditor
    PUSH_ACTION     StartMyEditor
    ICON            MyEd
}
```

▼ *To Create a Client Window Control*

A client window control is an application window embedded in the Front Panel. For example, you can put a system load meter in the Front Panel by creating an `xload` client window control.

1. Define the control.

   Use these fields to define the control's behavior:

   - `TYPE`: Set to `client`.
   - `CLIENT_NAME`: Specifies the client to be started.

     The value of `CLIENT_NAME` must match the first string (*res_name*) in the WM_CLASS properly on the application's top-level window. For more information, see the `xprop(1)` man page.
   - `CLIENT_GEOMETRY`: Specifies the size, in pixels, needed for the client's Front Panel window.

     The `xwininfo(1)` man page describes how to find out the size of a window in pixels.

2. Choose Restart Workspace Manager from the Workspace menu.

3. Start the client from a terminal emulator command line.

For example, the following control displays a 30 × 20 pixel load meter.

```
CONTROL LoadMeter
{
    TYPE            client
```

```
    CONTAINER_NAME Top
    CONTAINER_TYPE BOX
    CLIENT_NAME    xload
    CLIENT_GEOMETRY30x20
}
```

If the client is not saved and restored between sessions, you may want to configure the control to start the client when the user clicks it. For example, you can configure the LoadMeter control to start `xload` by adding the following line to the definition:

```
PUSH_ACTION    StartXload
```

and creating the action:

```
ACTION StartXload
{
    WINDOW_TYPE    NO_STDIO
    EXEC_STRING    /usr/contrib/bin/X11/xload
}
```

▼ To Animate a Control

You can attach an animation sequence to be used when the user chooses the control or drops an object on it.

In order to have an animation sequence, a control must:

- Be type `icon`
- Have a `PUSH_ACTION` or `DROP_ACTION`

1. Specify the animation sequence using the `ANIMATION` component:

   ```
   ANIMATION animation_name
   {
    icon_image           [delay]
    icon_image           [delay]
    ...
   }
   ```

   where *delay* is the time delay between animation icons, in milliseconds.

2. Add the `PUSH_ANIMATION` and/or `DROP_ANIMATION` fields to the control definition. The value is the name of the `ANIMATION` sequence.

For example, the following lines animate a control that starts the BestEditor application. The time delay between icons is 300 milliseconds. The example assumes you've created icon files `frame1`, `frame2`, etc.

```
CONTROL BestEditor
{
    ...
    PUSH_ANIMATION BestEdAnimation
    ...
}

ANIMATION BestEdAnimation
{
    frame1      300
    frame2
    ...
}
```

Providing On Item Help for Front Panel Controls

There are two ways to provide help for a control:

- Providing a help sting in the control definition.

  The help string is displayed in the help viewer when the user invokes on-item help for the control. The help string cannot include formatting (such as headings) or links.

  To provide a help string, specify the help string in the control definition:

  `HELP_STRING` *help_string*

- Specifying a help topic in a registered help volume.

  A help topic is information authored using the full capabilities of the help system. Authoring a help topic requires you to use the desktop Help Developer's Kit.

  To provide a help topic, specify the help volume and topic ID in the control definition:

  `HELP_VOLUME` *help_volume_name*
  `HELP_TOPIC` *topic_id*

Customizing the Workspace Switch

There are several ways to customize the workspace switch:

- Changing the number of workspaces
- Changing the layout of the switch
- Changing the controls in the switch

▼ To Change the Default Number of Workspaces

♦ Modify the following Workspace Manager resource:

```
Dtwm*workspaceCount: n
```

For more information, see "To Change the Number of Workspaces on a System-Wide Basis" on page 244.

▼ To Change the Number of Switch Rows

♦ Modify the `NUMBER_OF_ROWS` field in the `SWITCH` definition.

For example, the following definition defines a three-row switch.

```
SWITCH Switch
{
    CONTAINER_NAME box_name
    NUMBER_OF_ROWS 3
  ...
}
```

▼ To Change or Add Controls in the Workspace Switch

1. Create a Front Panel configuration file with the control definition.
   - Specify that the control be inside the switch:

     ```
     CONTAINER_NAME    Switch
     CONTAINER_TYPE    SWITCH
     ```

   - Specify the position in the switch:

     ```
     POSITION_HINTS     n
     ```

     where *n* is an integer. The positions are numbered sequentially left-to-right, top-to-bottom. (For the default two-row switch, the positions are 1 through 4.)

2. Create the icon for the control. The recommended size is 16 by 16 pixels.

For example, the following control puts a Terminal control in the switch.

```
CONTROL SwitchTerminal
{
  TYPE                  icon
  CONTAINER_NAME        Switch
  CONTAINER_TYPE        SWITCH
  POSITION_HINTS        3
  ICON                  Fpterm
  LABEL                 Terminal
  PUSH_ACTION           Dtterm
  HELP_TOPIC            FPOnItemTerm
  HELP_VOLUME           FPanel
}
```

The control uses a built-in icon and the same help topic used by the Terminal control in the Personal Applications subpanel.

General Front Panel Configuration

Front Panel's PANEL syntax allows you to:

- Change the location of the Front Panel
- Change the window decoration
- Set general appearance and behavior of controls

The default PANEL description is in /usr/dt/appconfig/types/*language*/dtwm.fp.

For additional information, see the dtfpfile(4X) man page.

General Steps

1. Create a new Front Panel configuration file in /etc/dt/appconfig/types/*language* or *HomeDirectory*/.dt/types.

2. Copy the default PANEL description from /usr/dt/types/*language*/dtwm.fp to the new file.

3. Edit the PANEL description.

The new PANEL description has precedence over the default one.

To Change the Default Front Panel Location

♦ Use the PANEL_GEOMETRY field in the PANEL definition to specify the location.

For example, the following panel is in the upper right corner.

```
PANEL SpecialFrontPanel
{
  PANEL_GEOMETRY       -1+1
   …
}
```

To Label Controls in the Main Panel

1. Add the following line to the PANEL definition:

```
DISPLAY_CONTROL_LABELS    True
```

2. Add a LABEL field to each control.

The *control_name* is used if no LABEL is specified.

To Change the Click Behavior of Controls

♦ Use the CONTROL_BEHAVIOR field in the PANEL definition to specify how the user runs a control's PUSH_ACTION. Values for the field are:

single_click	The user clicks the control to run the PUSH_ACTION
double_click	The user double-clicks the control to run the PUSH_ACTION

To Create an Entirely New Front Panel

Creating a new Front Panel may be preferable when you want to make extensive changes.

To avoid conflict with the built-in Front Panel components, an entirely new Front Panel should use new names for the PANEL and other containers.

1. Create the PANEL component for the new Front Panel. Give it a unique name:

   ```
   PANEL front_panel_name
   {
       ...
   }
   ```

2. Create the new boxes and controls, using the new container names.

   If you want to use existing components, you must copy their definitions and change the CONTAINER_NAME value.

3. Choose Restart Workspace Manager from the Workspace menu.

Example of Creating a Personal Front Panel with Three Rows

The following example changes the default Front Panel so that its controls are organized into three rows.

1. Copy /usr/dt/appconfig/types/*language*/dtwm.fp to *HomeDirectory*/.dt.types/MyFrontPanel.fp. Give the file write permission.

   This is the file you will edit to provide the new Front Panel.

2. Change the name of the Front Panel:

   ```
   PANEL NewFrontPanel
   ```

3. Change the name of the box named Top and edit its container name:

   ```
   BOX NewFrontPanelTop
   {
     CONTAINER_NAMENewFrontPanel
     POSITION_HINTSfirst
     ...
   }
   ```

4. Add box definitions for the middle and bottom rows:

   ```
   BOX NewFrontPanelMiddle
   {
     CONTAINER_NAME    NewFrontPanel
     POSITION_HINTS    second
   }
   ```

```
BOX NewFrontPanelBottom
{
  CONTAINER_NAME     NewFrontPanel
  POSITION_HINTS     second
}
```

5. Change the `CONTAINER_NAME` of the following controls to `NewFrontPanelTop`:
   - Clock
   - Date
   - Home
   - TextEditor
   - Mail
6. Change the `CONTAINER_NAME` of the following controls to `NewFrontPanelBottom`:
   - Printer
   - Style
   - Applications
   - Help
   - Trash
7. Change the `CONTAINER_NAME` of the switch to `NewFrontPanelMiddle`.
8. Set the resource:

   ```
   Dtwm*frontPanel*name:  NewFrontPanel
   ```
9. Choose Restart Workspace Manager from the Workspace menu.

Customizing the Workspace Manager 14

This chapter describes how to customize the desktop Workspace Manager.

The Workspace Manager is the window manager provided by the desktop. Like other window managers, it controls:

- The appearance of window frame components
- The behavior of windows, including their stacking order and focus behavior
- Key bindings and button bindings
- The appearance of minimized windows
- Workspace and Window menus

In addition, the Workspace Manager controls these desktop components:

- *Workspaces*. The Workspace Manager controls the number of workspaces, and keeps track of which windows are open in each workspace.

- *Workspace backdrops.* The user changes backdrops using Style Manager. However, backdrop management is a function of the Workspace Manager.
- *The Front Panel.* Although the Front Panel uses its own configuration files, it is created and managed by the Workspace Manager.

Many of these can be changed with Style Manager. Style Manager is able to make often-used changes quickly, with little effort on your part. Other resources must be set manually.

The Workspace Manager is `dtwm`. It is based on the OSF/Motif Window Manager.

See Also

- For reference information about the Workspace Manager, see the `dtwm(1)` and `dtwmrc(4)` man pages.
- For information about setting Workspace Manager resources, see "Setting Application Resources" on page 256.
- For information on Front Panel configuration files, see Chapter 13, "Advanced Front Panel Customization."

For additional information about setting resources, see "Setting Application Resources" on page 256.

Workspace Manager Configuration Files

The Workspace Manager gets information about the window menus, workspace menus, button bindings, and key bindings from a configuration file.

It uses one of the following files:

- Personal file: *HomeDirectory*`/.dt/dtwmrc`
- System custom file: `/etc/dt/config/`*language*`/sys.dtwmrc`
- Built-in file: `/usr/dt/config/`*language*`/sys.dtwmrc`

The Workspace Manager searches for a configuration file in the order shown above, and uses the first one it finds.

For users who use more than one session language, a personal, language-dependent configuration file *HomeDirectory*`/.dt/`*language*`/dtwrmc` can be created that takes precedence over *HomeDirectory*`/.dt/dtwmrc`.

▼ To Create or Modify a Personal Configuration File

The personal Workspace Manager configuration file is *HomeDirectory*/.dt/dtwmrc. If this file exists, it is the file used.

1. Double-click Edit Dtwmrc in the Desktop_Tools application group.

   If you already have a personal dtwmrc file, it is loaded into the editor. If not, sys.dtwmrc is copied to *HomeDirectory*/.dt/dtwmrc, which is then loaded into the editor.

2. Edit the file.

3. Exit the editor.

   The file is saved as your personal dtwmrc, regardless of its original source.

▼ To Create a System-Wide Configuration File

The system-wide Workspace Manager configuration file is /etc/dt/config/*language*/sys.dtwmrc.

♦ Copy /usr/dt/config/*language*/sys.dtwmrc to /etc/dt/config/*language*/sys.dtwmrc.

Note – This file is not used if *HomeDirectory*/.dt/dtwmrc exists.

▼ To Include (Source In) Other Files

♦ Use the syntax:

```
include
{
   path
   path
   ...
}
```

For example, the following lines source in the file /users/ellen/mymenu:

```
include
{
   /users/ellen/mymenu
}
```

Include statements are useful for providing additional functionality without copying the entire configuration file. For example, a user might want to create a new key binding without having to administer the entire configuration file. The user can create a file *HomeDirectory*/.dt/dtwmrc with this content:

```
include
{
 /etc/dt/config/C/sys.dtwmrc
}
Keys DtKeyBindings
{
  Alt<Key>F5 root  f.menu  Applications
}
Menu Applications
{
  "GraphicsApp" f.exec "/usr/bin/GraphicsApp/GApp"
  ...
}
```

▼ To Restart the Workspace Manager

The Workspace Manager must be restarted in order for changes made to the configuration file to take effect.

- Choose Restart Workspace Manager from the Workspace menu (press mouse button 3 when the pointer is on the backdrop).

Customizing Workspaces

Most workspace customization, such as changing workspace names and the number of workspaces, can be done by the user using the desktop's interface. However, the Workspace Manager provides resources for setting system-wide defaults.

▼ To Change the Number of Workspaces on a System-Wide Basis

The default desktop configuration provides four workspaces. The user can add and delete workspaces using the pop-up menu associated with the Workspace switch.

The Workspace Manager provides a resource for changing the default number of workspaces.

♦ Use the `workspaceCount` resource to set the number of workspaces:

```
Dtwm*workspaceCount: number
```

For information about setting Workspace Manager resources, see "Setting Application Resources" on page 256.

For example, the following resource sets the number of workspaces to six:

```
Dtwm*workspaceCount: 6
```

▼ To Provide System-Wide Workspace Names

Internally, the workspaces are numbered by the numbering convention `wsn`, where *n* is 0, 1, 2, and so on. For example, the default four workspaces are numbered internally `ws0` through `ws3`.

♦ Use the `title` resource to change the name of a specified workspace:

```
Dtwm*wsn: name
```

For information about setting Workspace Manager resources, see "Setting Application Resources" on page 256.

For example, the following resources set the default four workspaces to the specified names:

```
Dtwm*ws0*title:  Anna
Dtwm*ws1*title:  Don
Dtwm*ws2*title   Julia
Dtwm*ws3*title   Patti
```

▼ To Create Additional Backdrops

1. Create the backdrop images. They can be bitmap or pixmap files.
2. Place the backdrops in one of the following directories. (You may have to create the directory.)
   - System-wide backdrops: `/etc/dt/backdrops`
   - Personal backdrops: *HomeDirectory*`/.dt/backdrops`
3. Choose Restart Workspace Manager from the Workspace menu.

The system-wide and personal backdrops are added to the built-in backdrops in `/usr/dt/backdrops`.

You can replace an existing built-in backdrop by creating a personal or system-wide backdrop with the same name.

▼ To Replace the Backdrop With a Graphics Image

The backdrops are layered over the display's root window. The Style Manager Backdrop dialog box provides a NoBackdrop setting in which the backdrop is transparent.

There is only one root window behind all the workspace backdrops. Thus, a graphics image placed on the root window persists across all workspaces. You can specify which workspaces cover up the root window with a backdrop. However, the image visible when NoBackdrop is in effect will be the same for every workspace.

1. Create the graphics image. It must be in a format for which a tool exists to display the image on the root window. For example, if you intend to use `xsetroot`, you must create a bitmap file.
2. If it doesn't already exist, create an executable file *HomeDirectory*`/.dt/sessions/sessionetc`. The `sessionetc` file is run each time the user logs in.
3. Place the command to display the image in the `sessionetc` file.

   For example, the following command tiles the root window with the specified bitmap:

   ```
   xsetroot -bitmap /users/ellen/.dt/icons/root.bm
   ```

Workspace Manager Menus

Workspace Manager has three default menus:

Workspace menu	Also called the root menu. Displayed when the user presses mouse button 3 when the pointer is on the backdrop. The menu is associated with the mouse button through a button binding.

Window menu — The menu displayed when the user presses mouse buttons 1 or 3 when the pointer is on the Window menu button (upper left corner of the window frame). The menu is associated with the button by the `windowMenu` resource.

Front Panel menu — The menu displayed when the user presses mouse buttons 1 or 3 when the pointer is over the Front Panel's Window menu button.

Workspace Manager Menu Syntax

Workspace Manager menus have the syntax:

```
Menu MenuName
{
    selection1  [mnemonic]  [accelerator] function [argument]
    selection2  [mnemonic]  [accelerator] function [argument]
    ...
}
```

where:

selection — The text or bitmap that appears on the menu. If the text includes spaces, enclose the text in quotation marks. For bitmaps, use the syntax @*/path*.

mnemonic — A single character that acts as a keyboard shortcut when the menu is displayed. It is specified in the form *_character.*

accelerator — A keyboard shortcut that is active whether or not the menu is displayed. Accelerators have the syntax *modifier*`<Key>` *Keyname* where modifier is `Ctrl`, `Shift`, `Alt` (Extend char), or `Lock`. For a list of all possible key names, refer to the `keysymdef.h` file in your "X11 include" directory.

function — The function to be performed when this selection is made. Refer to the `dtwmrc(4)` man page for a list of functions.

argument — Function arguments. Refer to the `dtwmrc(4)` man page for more details.

For example, the following menu item labeled Restore normalizes the window. When the menu is displayed, typing "R" will also restore the window. Pressing Extend char F5 will also restore the window.

```
Restore    _R    Alt<Key> F5    f.normalize
```

Note – For complete information on Workspace Manager menu syntax, see the `dtwmrc(4)` man page.

▼ To Modify the Existing Workspace (Root) Menu

1. Open the appropriate file for editing:
   - Personal: *HomeDirectory*`/.dt/dtwmrc`
   - System-wide: `/etc/dt/config/`*language*`/sys.dtwmrc`

   For information on creating these files, see "Workspace Manager Configuration Files" on page 242.

2. Edit the description of the Workspace menu.

   The default Workspace menu is named DtRootMenu.

```
Menu DtRootMenu
{
    "Workspace Menu"                    f.title
    "Shuffle Up"                        f.circle_up
    "Shuffle Down"                      f.circle_down
    ...
}
```

▼ To Create a New Workspace (Root) Menu

1. Open the appropriate file for editing:
   - Personal: *HomeDirectory*`/.dt/dtwmrc`
   - System-wide: `/etc/dt/config/`*language*`/sys.dtwmrc`

   For information on creating these files, see "Workspace Manager Configuration Files" on page 242.

2. Create the new menu:

```
Menu menu_name
{
        ...
}
```

   See "Workspace Manager Menu Syntax" on page 247.

3. Create or edit the button binding to display the new menu.

If the menu replaces the existing menu, edit the button binding that displays the Workspace menu.

```
<Btn3Down> root  f.menu  menu_name
```

If the menu is an additional menu, create a new mouse button binding. For example, the following button binding displays the menu when Shift-mouse button 3 is pressed over the backdrop:

```
Shift<Btn3Down> root  f.menu  menu_name
```

4. Choose Restart Workspace Manager from the Workspace menu.

▼ To Create a New Window Menu

Note – The Window menu is built into the Workspace Manager, and ordinarily is not customized. To keep window behavior consistent between applications, you should avoid extensive modification to the Window menu.

---

1. Open the appropriate file for editing:
   - Personal: *HomeDirectory*`/.dt/dtwmrc`
   - System-wide: `/etc/dt/config/`*language*`/sys.dtwmrc`

   For information on creating these files, see "Workspace Manager Configuration Files" on page 242.

2. Create the new menu:

```
Menu menu_name
{
        ...
}
```

3. Use the `windowMenu` resource to specify the new menu:

```
Dtwm*windowMenu: menu_name
```

4. Choose Restart Workspace Manager from the Workspace menu.

Customizing Button Bindings

A *button binding* associates a mouse button operation and possible keyboard modifier key with a window manager function. Button bindings apply to all workspaces.

The desktop default button bindings are defined in the Workspace Manager configuration file in a button binding set named `DtButtonBindings`:

```
Buttons DtButtonBindings
{
  ...
}
```

Button Binding Syntax

The syntax for button bindings is:

```
Buttons ButtonBindingSetName
{
     [modifier]<button_nameMouse_action>  context function  [argument]
     [modifier]<button_nameMouse_action>  context function  [argument]
```

where:

button_name
`Btn1`–Left mouse button
`Btn2`–Middle button (3-button mouse) or both buttons (2-button mouse)
`Btn3`–Right button
`Btn4`–Buttons 1 and 2 together on a 3-button mouse
`Btn5`–Buttons 2 and 3 together on a 3-button mouse

modifier
`Ctrl, Shift, Alt, Lock`

mouse_action
`Down`—Holding down a mouse button
`Up`—Releasing a mouse button
`Click`—Pressing and releasing a mouse button
`Click2`—Double-clicking a mouse button
`Drag`—Dragging the mouse while holding down the mouse button

context — Indicates where the pointer must be for the binding to be effective. If necessary, separate multlple contents with the "|" character.

`root`—The workspace window
`window`—Client window or window frame
`frame`–Window frame, excluding the contents
`icon`–Icon
`title`–Title bar
`app`–Client window (excluding the frame)

function — One of the window manager functions. Refer to the `dtwmrc(4)` man page for a list of valid functions.

argument — Any window manager function arguments that are required. Refer to the `dtwmrc(4)` man page for details.

For example, the following line causes the menu described in `DtRootMenu` to be displayed when mouse button 3 is pressed while the pointer is in the workspace window (but not within client windows).

```
<Btn3Down>        root        f.menu        DtRootMenu
```

Note – For complete information on button binding syntax, see the `dtwmrc(4)` man page.

▼ To Add a Button Binding

1. Open the appropriate file for editing:
   - Personal: *HomeDirectory*`/.dt/dtwmrc`
   - System-wide: `/etc/dt/config/`*language*`/sys.dtwmrc`

   For information on creating these files, see "Workspace Manager Configuration Files" on page 242.

2. Add the button binding to the `DtButtonBindings` definition.

   Do not bind the same button to different functions for the click and press operations, and do not bind more than one function to the same button and context.

3. Choose Restart Workspace Manager from the Workspace menu.

▼ To Create a New Button Binding Set

1. Open the appropriate file for editing:
   - Personal: *HomeDirectory*`/.dt/dtwmrc`
   - System-wide: `/etc/dt/config/`*language*`/sys.dtwmrc`

   For information on creating these files, see "Workspace Manager Configuration Files" on page 242.

2. Create the new button binding set. See "Button Binding Syntax" on page 250.

3. Set the `buttonBindings` resource to the new name:

   `Dtwm*buttonBindings:` *ButtonBindingsSetName*

4. Choose Restart Workspace Manager from the Workspace menu.

Note – The new button bindings replace your existing button bindings. Copy any button bindings you want to keep from `DtButtonBindings`.

Customizing Key Bindings

A *keyboard binding*, also known as a *key binding*, associates combination of keys with Workspace Manager functions. Key bindings apply to all workspaces.

Note – Be careful about using a common key combination as a keyboard binding. For example, Shift-A normally puts the letter "A" into your current window. If you bind Shift-A to a function, you lose its normal usage.

Default Desktop Key Bindings

The desktop default key bindings are defined in the Workspace Manager configuration file in a key binding set named `DtKeyBindings`:

```
Keys DtKeyBindings
{
 ...
}
```

Key Binding Syntax

The syntax for key bindings is:

```
Keys KeyBindingSetName
{
    [Modifiers]<Key>key_name  context  function  [argument]
    [Modifiers]<Key>key_name  context  function  [argument]
    ...
}
```

where:

Modifiers — Ctrl, Shift. Alt, and Lock. Multiple modifiers are allowed; separate them with spaces.

key_name — The key to which the function is mapped. For keys with letters or numbers, the *key_name* name is usually printed on the key. For instance the name of the "a" key is "a", and the "2" key is named "2". The "Tab" key is named "Tab". The "F3" key is named "F3".

For other keys, the name is spelled out—for example, plus for the "+" key. The file keysymdef.h, located in a system-dependent directory, contains additional information about key names.

context — The element that must have the keyboard focus for this action to be effective. These can be concatenated together if the binding applies to more than one context. Multiple contexts are separated by the "|" character.

root–Workspace backdrop
window–Client window
icon–Icon

function — A window manager function. Refer to the dtwmrc(4) man page for a list of valid functions.

argument — Any window manager function arguments that are required. Refer to the dtwmrc(4) man page for details.

For example, the following key binding lets the user to switch the keyboard focus to the next transient window in an application by pressing Alt+F6.

```
Alt<Key>F6      window      f.next_key      transient
```

Note – For complete information on key binding syntax, see the `dtwmrc(4)` man page.

▼ To Create a Custom Key Binding Set

1. Open the appropriate file for editing:
   - Personal: *HomeDirectory*/`.dt/dtwmrc`
   - System-wide: `/etc/dt/config/`*language*`/sys.dtwmrc`

   For information on creating these files, see "Workspace Manager Configuration Files" on page 242.

1. Create a new key binding set with a unique *KeyBindingSetName*. Use the desktop default key binding set, `DtKeyBindings`, as a guide.

2. Set the `keyBindings` resource to the new set name:

   `Dtwm*keyBindings:` *KeyBindingSetName*

3. Choose Restart Workspace Manager from the Workspace menu.

Note – The new key bindings replace your existing key bindings. Copy any key bindings you want to keep from `DtKeyBindings` into your new set.

Switching Between Default and Custom Behavior

To toggle between OSF/Motif 1.2 default and CDE desktop window behavior:

1. Press Alt+Shift+Ctrl+!

2. Click OK in the dialog box.

Switching to default behavior removes the Front Panel and any custom key and button bindings.

Administering Application Resources, Fonts, and Colors

15

You can choose a wide range of colors and fonts for your display either by using Style Manager or by customizing additional font and color resources. This chapter discusses how to customize fonts and color resources.

This chapter also describes how to specify style translations for `DtEditor` widget applications such as the desktop text editor (`dtpad`) and Mailer (`dtmail`), and alternates for `DtEditor` widget application menu accelerators that conflict with these translations.

Setting Application Resources

Resources are used by applications to set certain aspects of appearance and behavior. For example, Style Manager (`dtstyle`) provides resources that enable you to specify where the system looks for files containing information about color palettes:

```
dtstyle*paletteDirectories: /usr/dt/palettes/C \ HomeDirectory/.dt/palettes
```

App-default files for the desktop applications are located in the `/usr/dt/app-defaults/`*language* directory.

▼ To Set System-Wide Resources

♦ Add the resources to the file `/etc/dt/config/`*language*`/sys.resources`. (You may have to create the file.)

For example, if in `/etc/dt/config/C/sys.resources` you specify:

```
AnApplication*resource: value
```

then the resource `AnApplication*resource` will be set in each user's RESOURCE_MANAGER property at the next login.

▼ To Set Personal Resources

1. Add the resources to the file *HomeDirectory*`/.Xdefaults`.
2. Double-click Reload Resources in the Desktop_Tools application group.

How the Desktop Loads Resources

Resources are loaded at session start-up by Session Manager. For information on how Session Manager loads the resources into the RESOURCE_MANAGER, see "Loading the Session Resources" on page 29.

Defining UNIX Bindings

By default UNIX bindings are not enabled.

▼ To Specify-EMACS Style Translations

The following procedure specifies:

- EMACS style translations for `DtEditor` widget applications such as the desktop Text Editor (`dtpad`) and Mailer (`dtmail`)
- Alternates for `DtEditor` widget application menu accelerators that conflict with these translations.

1. Add the following line to the *HomeDirectory*/`.Xdefaults` file:

   `#include "/usr/dt/app-defaults/`*language*`/UNIXbindings"`

   where *language* is the value of the LANG environment variable.

2. Restart your session.

▼ To Modify the EMACS-Style Translations

1. Insert the contents of the file `/usr/dt/app-defaults/`*language*`/UNIXbindings` into *HomeDirectory*/`.Xdefaults`.
2. Edit the bindings in the `.Xdefaults` file.
3. Restart your session when you have finished.

UNIX Bindings Provided by the UNIXbindings File

The `/usr/dt/app-defaults/`*language*`/UNIXbindings` file provides the following bindings:

Note – The Delete key deletes the previous character when the UNIX bindings are enabled, and Shift-Delete deletes the next character.

- Table 15-1 lists the `dtpad` overrides for menu accelerators and accelerator text that conflict with the UNIX bindings.

Table 15-1 `dtpad` Overrides for

Menu Accelerators and Accelerator Text	Override
`Dtpad*fileMenu.print.acceleratorText:`	
`Dtpad*fileMenu.print.accelerator:`	
`Dtpad*editMenu.undo.acceleratorText:`	Ctrl+_
`Dtpad*editMenu.undo.accelerator:`	Ctrl<Key>_
`Dtpad*editMenu.paste.acceleratorText:`	Shift+Insert
`Dtpad*editMenu.paste.accelerator:`	Shift<Key>osfInsert
`Dtpad*editMenu.selectAll.acceleratorText:`	Ctrl+/
`Dtpad*editMenu.selectAll.accelerator:`	Ctrl<Key>/

- Table 15-2 lists the `dtmail` Compose window overrides for menu accelerators and accelerator text that conflict with the UNIX bindings.

Table 15-2 `dtmail` Compose Window Overrides

Menu Accelerators and Accelerator Text	Override
`Dtmail*ComposeDialog*menubar*Edit.Undo.acceleratorText:`	Ctrl+_
`Dtmail*ComposeDialog*menubar*Edit.Undo.accelerator:`	Ctrl<Key>_
`Dtmail*ComposeDialog*menubar*Edit.Paste.acceleratorText:`	Shift+Insert
`Dtmail*ComposeDialog*menubar*Edit.Paste.accelerator:`	Shift<Key>osfInsert
`Dtmail*ComposeDialog*menubar*Edit.Find/Change.acceleratorText:`	Ctrl+S
`Dtmail*ComposeDialog*menubar*Edit.Find/Change.accelerator:`	Ctrl<Key>s

- The following translations provide (GNU style) EMACS control and meta key bindings plus some additional bindings. When appropriate, they also allow the Shift key to be used in combination with the normal binding to reverse the direction of the operation. For example, Ctrl+Shift+F will move the cursor backward a character since Ctrl+F normally moves it forward a character.

The additional bindings are:

Ctrl+comma	backward-word
Ctrl+Shift+comma	forward-word
Ctrl+period	forward-word
Ctrl+Shift+period	backward-word
Ctrl+Return	end-of-file
Ctrl+Shift+Return	beginning-of-file

GNU EMACS binds delete-previous-character() rather than delete-next-character() to the Delete key. Meta+F is normally the mnemonic for the File menu, so the binding to forward-word() will be ignored. Use one of the other bindings for forward-word (for example, Ctrl+period).

- Table 15-3 lists the `DtEditor.text` Translations.

Table 15-3 `DtEditor.text` Translations

Modifier Key	Key	Action Routine
c ~s	<Key>a:	beginning-of-line()\n\
c s	<Key>a:	end-of-line()\n\
c ~s	<Key>b:	backward-character()\n\
c s	<Key>b:	forward-character()\n\
c ~s	<Key>b:	backward-character()\n\
c s	<Key>b:	backward-word()\n\
m ~s	<Key>b:	backward-word()\n\
m s	<Key>b:	forward-word()\n\
c ~s	<Key>d:	delete-next-character()\n\
c s	<Key>d:	delete-previous-character()\n\
m ~s	<Key>d:	kill-next-word()\n\
m s	<Key>d:	kill-previous-word()\n\
c ~s	<Key>e:	end-of-line()\n\
c s	<Key>e:	beginning-of-line()\n\

Table 15-3 `DtEditor.text` Translations *(Continued)*

Modifier Key	Key	Action Routine
c ~s	<Key>f:	forward-character()\n\
c s	<Key>f:	backward-character()\n\
m ~s	<Key>f:	forward-word()\n\
m s	<Key>f:	backward-word()\n\
c	<Key>j:	newline-and-indent()\n\
c ~s	<Key>k:	kill-to-end-of-line()\n\
c s	<Key>k:	kill-to-start-of-line()\n\
c	<Key>l:	redraw-display()\n\
c	<Key>m:	newline()\n\
c s	<Key>n:	process-up()\n\
c ~s	<Key>n:	process-down()\n\
c	<Key>o:	newline-and-backup()\n\
c ~s	<Key>p:	process-up()\n\
c s	<Key>p:	process-down()\n\
c ~s	<Key>u:	kill-to-start-of-line()\n\
c s	<Key>u:	kill-to-end-of-line()\n\
c ~s	<Key>v:	next-page()\n\
c s	<Key>v:	previous-page()\n\
m ~s	<Key>v:	previous-page()\n\
m s	<Key>v:	next-page()\n\
c	<Key>w:	kill-selection()\n\
c ~s	<Key>y:	unkill()\n\
m	<Key>]:	forward-paragraph()\n\
m	<Key>[:	backward-paragraph()\n\
c ~s	<Key>comma:	backward-word()\n\
c s	<Key>comma:	forward-word()\n\
m	<Key>\\<:	beginning-of-file()\n\

Table 15-3 `DtEditor.text` Translations *(Continued)*

Modifier Key	Key	Action Routine
c ~s	<Key>period:	forward-word()\n\
c s	<Key>period:	backward-word()\n\
m	<Key>\\>:	end-of-file()\n\
c ~s	<Key>Return:	end-of-file()\n\
c s	<Key>Return:	beginning-of-file()\n\
~c ~s ~m ~a	<Key>osfDelete:	delete-previous-character()\n\
~c s ~m ~a	<Key>osfDelete:	delete-next-character()

Administering Fonts

Using the Style Manager Font dialog box, you can select the font size you want for all applications. You can also specify fonts on the command line or use resources to:

- Set font resources for individual applications
- Assign different fonts to be used by the Font dialog box

A *font* is a type style in which text characters are printed or displayed. The desktop includes a variety of fonts in different styles and sizes.

A *bitmap font* is made from a matrix of dots. (By default, Style Manager configures bitmap fonts only.) The font is completely contained in one file. Many files are needed to have a complete range of sizes, slants, and weights.

Fonts are specified as values of resources and as parameters to commands. The X Logical Font Description (XLFD) name is the method by which a desired font is requested. The system finds the font that best matches the description it was given.

Setting Desktop Font Resources

The Style Manager Font dialog box enables you to set fonts (up to seven sizes) for things such as text entry and labels.

Resources Set by the Font Dialog Box

When a font is selected, the following resources are written to the RESOURCE_MANAGER property:

- `SystemFont` is used for system areas, such as menu bars, menu panes, push buttons, toggle buttons, and labels. The following resource is set by `SystemFont`:

`*FontList`	Displayed in system areas of desktop clients and other clients created using the OSF/Motif toolkit.

- `UserFont` is used for text entered into windows. The following resources are set by `UserFont`:

`*Font`	Supports earlier versions of X applications
`*FontSet`	The primary setting
`*XmText*FontList`	Displayed in text entry boxes
`*XmTextField*FontList`	Displayed in text entry boxes

Resources Used by the Font Dialog Box

The fonts used for each selection in the Font dialog box are specified in the `/usr/dt/app-defaults/Dtstyle` resource file. Up to seven sizes can be specified.

`NumFonts`	Number of font sizes in the Font dialog box
`SystemFont[1-7]`	Up to seven resources assigning a specific font to a Font dialog box selection for `SystemFont`
`UserFont[1-7]`	Up to seven resources assigning a specific font to a Font dialog box selection for `UserFont`

Note – The default fonts for these resources have been chosen for readability on various displays. If you want a specific font for an application, set the font with an application font resource rather than changing these desktop fonts.

For more information about application fonts, seethe `DtStdAppFontNames(5)` and `DtStdInterfaceFontNames(5)` man pages.

▼ To List Available Fonts

1. Type the following:

   `xlsfonts [-options] [-fn pattern]`

   A list of XLFD names and font alias names available on your system is displayed. Bitmap fonts show values in all fourteen XLFD fields. Scalable typefaces show zeros in the *PixelSize, PointSize, ResolutionX,* and *ResolutionY* positions.

2. To check for specific fonts, use the pattern-matching capability of `xlsfonts`. Use wildcards to replace the part of the pattern you are not trying to match.

3. If `xlsfonts` does not show any font names starting with `dt`, your font path does not include the desktop fonts. Type the following command to include the desktop fonts into your available fonts:

   `xset +fp directory name`

   where *directory name* is the directory containing the desktop fonts. The default location set by session startup is `/usr/dt/config/xfonts/`*language*.

For additional information, see:

- The `xset` and `xlsfonts` man pages list the available options.
- *Using the X Window System* explains font alias names and the `xset` client.

▼ To Specify Fonts on the Command Line

♦ Use the `-xrm` command-line option to specify a font resource for a specific client. For example:

```
application name -xrm "*bitstream-charter-medium-r-normal-8-88-75-75-p-45-iso8859-1"
```

X Logical Font Description (XLFD)

A font is specified by listing fourteen different characteristics, separated by dashes (-). This is called the X Logical Font Description (XLFD). In some cases, a property in the list can be replaced by a * wildcard, and a character within a property can be replaced by a ? wildcard. Table 15-4 lists font property string specifications.

The form of the property string specification is:

"*-Foundry-FamilyName-WeightName-Slant-SetwidthName-AddStyleName-PixelSize-PointSize-ResolutionX-ResolutionY-Spacing-AverageWidth-CharSetRegistry-CharSetCoding*"

Table 15-4 Font Property String Specification

Property String	Definition
Foundry	A string identifying the font designer
FamilyName	A string identifying the trademarked name of the font
WeightName	A string giving the relative weight of the font, such as bold
Slant	A code describing the direction of slant R (Roman–no slant) I (Italic–slant right) O (Oblique–slant right) RI (Reverse Italic–slant left) RO (Reverse Oblique–slant left)
SetwidthName	A string describing the width, such as compressed or expanded
AddStyleName	A string providing any additional information needed to uniquely identify the font
PixelSize	An integer giving the size of an em-square in pixels
PointSize	An integer giving the size of an em-square in decipoints
ResolutionX	An integer giving the horizontal resolution in pixels
ResolutionY	An integer giving the vertical resolution in pixels
Spacing	A code specifying the spacing between units `M` (Monospace--fixed pitch) `P` (Proportional space--variable pitch) `C` (Character cell)
AverageWidth	An integer giving the average width in 1/10th pixels
CharSetRegistry	A string identifying the registration authority that has registered the font encoding
CharSetEncoding	A string identifying the character set in the specified registry

Example

The following XLFD name describes a font named `charter` made by Bitstream that supports the ISO8859-1 standard encoding:

```
-bitstream-charter-medium-r-normal--8-80-75-75-p-45-iso8859-1
```

It is medium weight, with no special slanting, and normal width. The font is proportional, with an em-square box of 8 pixels or 8.0 points. The horizontal and vertical resolution are both 75 pixels. The average width of a character is 45 1/10ths pixels or 4.5 pixels.

Parts of this string can be replaced by wildcards. The system uses the first font it finds that matches the parts you have specified.

If all you want is an eight-pixel `charter` font, you could use:

```
*-charter-*-*-*-*-8-*
```

Administering Colors

This section describes:

- How Style Manager sets display colors.
- Resources used by Style Manager to control desktop color usage.

Color Palettes

A palette consists a group of color sets. The color sets for the current palette are shown in the Style Manager Color dialog box

A file exists for each palette. The `paletteDirectories` resource specifies the directories containing palette files. By default, this resource contains:

- Built-in palettes: `/usr/dt/palettes`
- System-wide palettes: `/etc/dt/palettes`
- Personal palettes: *HomeDirectory*`/.dt/palettes`

Color Sets

Each color set in the current palette is represented by a color button in the Style Manager Color dialog box. Each color is identified by a color set ID—a number from 1 to 8.

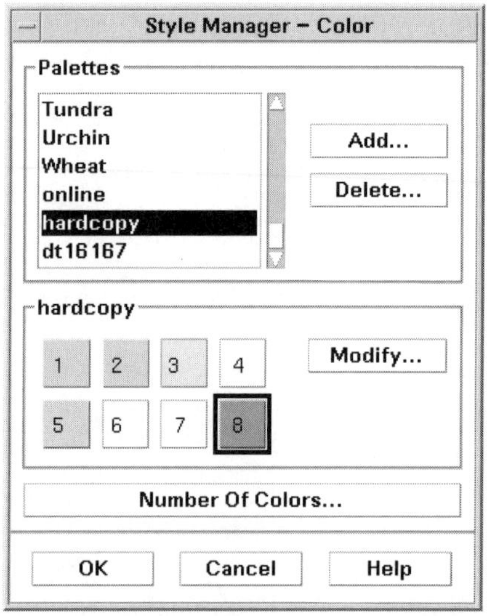

Figure 15-1 Color set ID values for HIGH_COLOR

Each color set is composed of up to five colors. Each color button displays the background color of the color set. The five colors in each color set represent the following display component resources:

`foreground`	The foreground of an application window or window frame. It is always black or white. This is generally used for text within windows and titles.
`background`	The background of the application or the window frame.
`topShadowColor`	The color of the top and left bevels of application controls (such as push buttons) and window frames.
`bottomShadowColor`	The color of the bottom and right bevels of application controls and window frames.

`selectColor`	The color that indicates the active state of certain controls, such as active toggles and buttons.

The number of color sets used by each palette is determined by the `colorUse` resource, which the user can set using the Style Manager Number of Colors To Use dialog box.

Specifying Color Values

Style Manager uses RGB values when writing color information to its palette files. The syntax for RGB numbers is:

#*RedGreenBlue*

Red, *Green*, and *Blue* are hexadecimal numbers, each 1 to 4 digits long, that indicate the amount of that color used. There must be the same number of digits for each of the colors. Thus, valid color values consist of 3, 6, 9, or 12 hexadecimal digits.

For example, white can be specified in any of the following ways:

```
#fff
#ffffff
#fffffffff
#ffffffffffff
```

If you set a color resource directly, you can use either the color name or RGB value. The file `/usr/lib/X11/rgb.txt` lists all the named colors.

How Color Sets are Mapped to Resources

The desktop maps color sets to various display elements through resources, and makes the following assignments:

Resource	Display element
`activeColorSetId`	Active window frame color
`inactiveColorSetId`	Inactive window frame color
`textColorSetId`	Text entry areas
`primaryColorSetId`	Application's main background areas
`secondaryColorSetId`	Application's menu bar, menus, and dialog boxes

These resources take a color set ID as their value. Coloring display elements with color set IDs allows the element to dynamically change to the new color scheme when a new palette is selected with Style Manager.

You can use these resources for individual applications. For example, the following line shows how you would visually group all `dtterm` windows by using color set 8 for their primary color.

```
dtterm*primaryColorSetId:   8
```

Default Color Set Assignments

The color set IDs used for display elements depends on the Number of Colors setting in Style Manager:

- High color (8 color sets)—Style Manager setting More Colors for Desktop:

Color set ID	Display element
1	Active window frame color
2	Inactive window frame color
3	Unused (by default)
4	Text entry areas
5	Application's main background areas
6	Application's menu bar, menus, and dialog boxes
7	Unused by default
8	Front Panel background

- Medium color (4 color sets)—Style Manager setting More Colors for Applications:

Color set ID	Display element
1	Active window frame color
2	Inactive window frame color
3	Application and Front Panel background color
4	Text entry areas

- Low color (2 color sets)—Style Manager setting Most Colors for Applications.

Color set ID	Display element
1	Active window frame, workspace selection buttons
2	All other display elements

Controlling Color with Style Manager

You can dynamically change color for desktop applications and other cooperating applications through Style Manager. The foreground and background colors set by Style Manager are available to non-cooperating applications.

- For a client to respond to Style Manager color changes, the client must be using the desktop Motif library. Clients written with other toolkits cannot change color dynamically in response to Style Manager changes. Color changes for these clients do not take effect until the client is restarted.
- There must be no other specific color resources applied for the client. This includes user-specified resources, appdefaults, and resources built into the application.
- Clients can specify `primaryColorSetId` and `secondaryColorSetId` resources to use certain colors within a desktop palette.

Number of Colors Used by Style Manager

The number of colors used by Style Manager depends on the values for the following resources:

`colorUse`	Configures the number of colors the desktop uses
`shadowPixmaps`	Directs the desktop to replace the two shadow colors with pixmaps
`foregroundColor`	Specifies if the foreground color changes dynamically.
`dynamicColor`	Controls whether applications change color when you switch palettes.

Table 15-5 lists the maximum number of colors allocated by the desktop.

Table 15-5 Number of Desktop Colors

Display	Maximum Number of Colors	Number Derived From
B_W	2	Black and white
LOW_COLOR	12	Two color sets times five colors plus black and white
MEDIUM_COLOR	22	Four color sets times five colors plus black and white
HIGH_COLOR	42	Eight color sets times five colors plus black and white

To determine the maximum number of colors:

1. Multiply the number of color sets in the palette by the number of colors within each color set.
2. Add 2 (for black and white).

However, with the following configuration you would only have ten colors in your palette: four color sets times two colors in each set (`background` and `selectColor`) plus black and white:

```
*colorUse:MEDIUM_COLOR
*shadowPixmaps: True
*foregroundColor:White
```

Note – Multi-color icons use fourteen additional colors.

colorUse Resource

The default value of the colorUse resource is MEDIUM_COLOR. The value of this resource affects the number of color sets used in a palette. Other resources affect the number of colors used to make shadows. The value of the colorUse resource also affects the use of multi-color icons.

Value	Description
B_W	"Black and White" Style Manager setting Displays with 1 to 3 color planes Number of color sets: 2 Maximum number of colors: 2 Default number of colors: 2 No multicolor icons
LOW_COLOR	"Most Color for Applications" Style Manager setting Displays with 4 to 5 color planes Number of color sets: 2 Maximum number of colors: 12 Default number of colors: 12 No multicolor icons
MEDIUM_COLOR	"More Colors for Application" Style Manager setting Displays with 6 color planes Number of color sets: 4 Maximum number of colors: 22 Default number of colors: 22 Multicolor icons
HIGH_COLOR	"More Colors for Desktop" Style Manager setting Displays with 7 or more color planes Number of color sets: 8 Maximum number of colors: 42 Default number of colors: 42 Multicolor icons\
default	The desktop chooses the correct value for that display. (To reduce the number of colors used by the desktop for high-color displays, the default colorUse resource is set to MEDIUM_COLOR.)

shadowPixmaps Resource

The shadowPixmaps resource directs the desktop to replace the two shadow colors with pixmaps. These pixmaps mix the background color with black or white to simulate top or bottom shadow values. This reduces the number of needed colors by two, since color cells do not need to be allocated for the shadow colors.

Value	Description
True	The desktop creates a topShadowPixmap and bottomShadowPixmap to use instead of the shadow colors.
False	topShadowColor and bottomShadowColor from the palette are used.

The default value for shadowPixmaps depends on the colorUse resource you have and the hardware support for the display.

foregroundColor Resource

The foregroundColor resource specifies how the foreground is configured in a palette.

Setting	Result
White	Foreground is set to white.
Black	Foreground is set to black.
Dynamic	(Default) Foreground is dynamically set to black or white, depending on the value of background. For instance, white letters on a yellow background are difficult to read, so the system chooses black.

If foregroundColor is set to either Black or White, the number of colors in the color set is reduced by one, and the foreground will not change in response to changes in the background color.

The default value for foregroundColor is Dynamic, except where the value of colorUse is B_W.

dynamicColor Resource

The `dynamicColor` resource controls whether applications change color dynamically; that is, whether the clients change color when you switch palettes.

Value	Description
True	Clients change color dynamically when a new palette is selected. This is the default value.
False	Clients do not change color dynamically. When a new palette is selected, clients will use the new colors when the session is restarted.

When the value of the `dynamicColor` resource is True, clients that cannot change colors dynamically (non-Motif applications) allocate different cells in the color map than clients that can change colors dynamically, even if you see the same color.

Note – Since all clients can share the same color cells, setting `dynamicColor` to False reduces the number of colors your desktop consumes.

Setting Shadow Thicknesses for Application Windows

The desktop defines a default shadow thickness of one pixel for the components in application windows, such as button shadows and focus highlight. Motif 1.2 applications use this resource value; other applications may not obtain this resource value and therefore will appear different on the display.

To set the shadow thickness to one pixel for non-Motif 1.2 applications:

1. Log in as root.
2. Create the `/etc/dt/config/`*language*`/sys.resources` file.
3. Specify the application-specific resource in `/etc/dt/config/`*language*`/sys.resources` as follows:

   application_class_name`*XmCascadeButton*shadowThickness: 1`

For more information about overriding system default resources and specifying additional resources for all desktop users, see "Loading the Session Resources" on page 29

Configuring Localized Desktop Sessions 16

To configure localized desktop sessions, you will need to:

- Set the LANG environment variable and other National Language Support (NLS) environment variables
- Access language-dependent message catalogs and resource files
- Execute applications remotely across internationalized systems

Managing the LANG Environment Variable

The LANG environment variable must be set for the desktop to use the operating system's language-sensitive routines. The desktop supports:

- Western Europe, Latin-based languages
- Japanese
- Traditional Chinese
- Simplified Chinese
- Korean

Note – Support for other languages may have been added by your desktop vendor.

You can set LANG to any value supported by the operating system. The Options menu in the login screen displays the list of supported languages and territories.

There are four ways to set LANG for the desktop:

- By editing a resource in the `Xconfig` file
- Using the Options menu in the login screen
- By creating an executable `sh` or `ksh` `Xsession.d` script. (See"Sourcing Xsession.d Scripts" on page 26 for more information about using an Xsession.d script.)
- By editing the user's `.dtprofile` file

When LANG is set, the desktop uses the following language-dependent files to determine the localized interface.

Colors	`/usr/dt/palettes/desc.`*language*
Backdrops	`/usr/dt/backdrops/desc.`*language*

Setting the Language for Multiple Users

If you set the language by means of an `Xconfig` file, the login screen is localized and LANG is set for all users. This is the only way to change LANG for all displays in multi-display systems. (To modify `Xconfig`, copy `/usr/dt/config/Xconfig` to `/etc/dt/config/Xconfig.`)

The language is set by placing the following line in `/etc/dt/config/Xconfig`:

`dtlogin.`*host_display*`.language:` *language*

For example, the following line sets LANG to `Swedish_locale` on display `my_host:0`.

```
dtlogin.my_host_0.language: Swedish_locale
```

The `dtlogin` client reads the appropriate message catalog for that language and brings up the localized login screen. The `dtlogin` client then determines the list of locales using the following resources in the `/etc/dt/config/Xresources` resource file:

- `dtlogin*language`
- `dtlogin*languageList`
- `dtlogin*languageName`

The `Xconfig` file may need to set the NLSPATH environment variable appropriately for the chosen language. If this is not the case, or if you want to set NLSPATH yourself, see "NLSPATH Environment Variable" on page 278.

Setting the Language for One Session

To set the language for one session, use the login screen Options menu. The login screen is localized and LANG is set for the user. LANG returns to its default value (set in `dtlogin`) at the conclusion of the session.

Setting the Language for One User

A user can override the login's LANG setting within the *HomeDirectory*`/.dtprofile` file. The login screen is not localized, and LANG is set for the user.

- If you use `sh` or `ksh`:

  `LANG=`*language*
  `export LANG`

- If you use `csh`:

  `setenv LANG` *language*

LANG Environment Variable and Session Configuration

The LANG environment variable changes the directory name that is searched for your session configuration files.

The localized session configuration files are:

- `/usr/dt/config/`*language*`/Xresources` (Login Manager resource file)
- `/usr/dt/config/`*language*`/sys.font` (Session Manager resource file)
- `/usr/dt/config/`*language*`/sys.resources` (Session Manager resource file)
- `/usr/dt/config/`*language*`/sys.session` (Session Manager executable shell)
- `/usr/dt/config/`*language*`/sys.dtwmrc` (Window Manager resource file)
- `/usr/dt/appconfig/types/`*language*`/dtwm.fp` (Window Manager Front Panel)

Setting Other NLS Environment Variables

Besides LANG, there are other NLS environment variables such as LC_CTYPE and LC_ALL. These variables are not affected by the `dtlogin` language resource nor by the login screen Options menu. They must be set in the following files:

- System-wide variables: `/etc/dt/config/Xsession.d`
- Personal variables: *HomeDirectory*`/.dtprofile`

NLSPATH Environment Variable

The NLSPATH environment variable determines the directory paths that applications search for message catalogs. Both LANG and NLSPATH must be set to use those message catalogs. Refer to "Localizing Message Catalogs" on page 282 for the location of localized messages. Most desktop clients will prefix the path to NLSPATH upon startup.

Finding Fonts

Fonts included with the desktop are in the `/usr/lib/X11/fonts` directory. Each directory contains a directory file, `fonts.dir`, and an alias file, `fonts.alias`. See the `mkfontdir` man page for information on creating the `fonts.dir` and `fonts.alias` files.

To list all fonts available at a server, user the `xlsfonts` command. To add or delete fonts to the server, use the `xset` command.

Localizing app-defaults Resource Files

The default location for the `app-defaults` file for the desktop clients is `/usr/dt/app-defaults/`*language*. For example, if LANG is set to `Swedish_locale`, then applications will look for their `app-defaults` file in `/usr/dt/app-defaults/Swedish_locale`. If LANG is not set, *language* is ignored, and applications look for their `app-defaults` file in `/usr/app-defaults/C`.

To change the location of `app-defaults`, use the XFILESEARCHPATH environment variable. For example, to move `app-defaults` to `/users`, set XFILESEARCHPATH to `/usr/app-defaults/`*language*/*classname*.

If you set XFILESEARCHPATH in *HomeDirectory*/`.dtprofile`, the value applies to all desktop and X clients you run. Nonclients will not find their resource files unless you link or copy them into the directory specified by XFILESEARCHPATH.

Localizing Actions and Data Types

Note – To customize a file in the `/usr/dt/appconfig` directory, copy the file to the `/etc/dt/appconfig` directory prior to customizing.

The search path for action and data-type definition files includes language-dependent directories in:

- Personal: *HomeDirectory*/`dt/types`
- System-wide: `/etc/dt/appconfig/types/`*language*
- Built-in: `/usr/dt/appconfig/types/`*language*

The search path for Application Manager's configuration files is:

- Personal: *HomeDirectory*/dt/appmanager
- System-wide: /etc/dt/appconfig/appmanager/*language*
- Built-in: /usr/dt/appconfig/appmanager/*language*

File and directory names in this directory are localized.

Localizing Icons and Bitmaps

To localize an icon, edit the icon with Icon Editor and save it in:

/etc/dt/appconfig/icons/*language*

If you save it in a different directory, set the XMICONSEARCHPATH environment variable to include the directory where you saved the icon. The XMICONBMSEARCHPATH environment variable controls the path used to search for icons.

Localizing Backdrop Names

Localization of backdrops is done through the use of description files (desc.*language* and desc.backdrops). No specific localized directory exists (such as /usr/dt/backdrops/*language*) for backdrop files. All locales use the same set of backdrops files but have their own desc.*language* file containing the translated names of the backdrops.

The description file contains resource specifications for the backdrop names that are translated. For example:

```
Backdrops*Corduroy.desc:  Velours
Backdrops*DarkPaper.desc: PapierKraft
Backdrops*Foreground.desc:AvantPlan
```

The desc.*language* file is used to retrieve the description of the backdrops for locale *language* in order to display the backdrop in the Style Manager. If there is a description specification, it will be displayed in the Style Manager backdrops list. Otherwise, the backdrop file name will be used.

Users can add their own backdrop descriptions in the *HomeDirectory*/.dt/backdrops/desc.backdrops file. This file is used to retrieve the backdrop descriptions for all backdrops added by the user regardless of locale.

The search path for the `description` files is:

- Personal: *HomeDirectory*`/.dt/backdrops/desc.backdrops`
- System-wide: `/etc/dt/backdrops/desc.`*language*
- Built-in: `/usr/dt/backdrops/desc.`*language*

Localizing Palette Names

Localization of palettes is done through the use of description files (`desc.`*language* and `desc.palettes`). No specific localized directory exists (such as `/usr/dt/palettes/`*language*). All locales use the same set of palette files but have their own `desc.palettes` file containing the translated names of the palettes.

The description file contains resource specifications for the palette names that are translated. For example:

```
Palettes*Cardamon.desc:    Cardamone
Palettes*Cinnamon.desc:    Cannelle
Palettes*Clove.desc:       Brun
```

The `desc.`*language* file is used to retrieve the description of the palettes for locale *language* in order to display the palette in the Style Manager list. If there is a description specification it will be displayed in the Style Manager palettes list. Otherwise, the palette file name will be used.

Users can add their own palette descirptions in the *HomeDirectory*`/.dt/palettes/desc.palettes` file. This file is used to retrieve the palette descriptions for all palettes added by the user regardless of locale.

The search path for the description files is:

- Personal: *HomeDirectory*`/.dt/palettes/desc.palettes`
- System-wide: `/etc/dt/palettes/desc.`*language*
- Built-in: `/usr/dt/palettes/desc.`*language*

Localizing Help Volumes

If you have localized a help volume, you must store it in one of the following directories. The first help volume found is the one used. The directories are searched in the following order:

- Personal: *HomeDirectory*`/.dt/help`
- System-wide: `/etc/dt/appconfig/help/`*language*
- Built-in: `/usr/dt/appconfig/help/`*language*

Localizing Message Catalogs

If you have localized a message catalog, store it in the following directory:

`/usr/dt/lib/nls/msg/`*language*.

These directories contain the `*.cat` files.

Executing Localized Desktop Applications Remotely

You can invoke localized desktop applications on any remote execution host that has a similarly localized desktop installation. The values of the NLS-related environment variables on the host that is invoking the application are passed to the remote host when the application is started. However, the environment variables do not contain any host information.

Resetting Your Keyboard Map

If you see unexpected characters and behaviors, or characters cannot be displayed or typed, you might need to reset or install your keyboard map or change your input method

.The input method is determined by the LC_CTYPE, LANG, or LC_ALL environment variables, or the language specified by the `-lang` option.

For example, if the user wants to open a terminal with the C locale within a POSIX shell, such as:

```
LANG=C   dtterm
```

This new terminal uses the C locale including the C input method and fonts. If you are using a language-specific keyboard, the input method may not accept any extended characters for input. When using the C locale with a language-specific keyboard, users need to set the LC_CTYPE (or LANG or LC_ALL)

environment variable to an appropriate value before invoking the terminal.

For example, to use the C locale with the German keyboard, type:

```
LANG=C LC_CTYPE=DeDE dtterm
```

If the X server has been reset and keymaps have been initialized, you can reset the proper keyboard map at the server using the `xmodmap` command.

Index

Symbols

%B, 115
%DatabaseHost%, 177
%DisplayHost%, 177
%H, 115
%L, 116
%LocalHost%, 177
%M, 116
%SessionHost%, 177
* wildcard character, 193
? wildcard character, 193

A

action definition file, created by Create Action, 142
action file, 142, 161
  contents, 132
  creating, 72, 161
  definition, 131
action icon, 131, 161, 162
  creating, 161
  required by desktop, 67
Action Icons controls, in Create Action, 145
Action Name field in Create Action, 145
action search path, See database search path
action servers, See database servers
actionIcon resource, 163
actions
  accepting dropped file or prompting, 169
  accepting dropped files, 134, 168
  accepting multiple dropped files, 172
  argument count restrictions, 175
  arguments, 167
  arguments, non-file, 169
  associating icon with, 205
  associating with data types, 191
  COMMAND, 156
  configuration files, 157
  creating icons for applications, 131
  creating manually, 155, 157, 158
  default icon, 163
  default terminal, 174
  different double-click and drop functionality, 176
  editing, 164
  environment variables, 179
  example, 159, 160
  execution string, 166
  fields, 158
  file arguments, 133
  files representing, See action file, 161

B

search path, 204
blank type control, 228
.bm filename extension, 202
bottomShadowColor resource, 266
BOX definition, 216
syntax, 217
BROADCAST, used in XDMCP-indirect, 9
browsing icons using File Manager, 207
busy type control, 229
button binding, 249
adding, 251
creating new set, 252
syntax, 250
buttonBindings resource, 252

C

Calendar daemon, 99
CDE-MIN files, 94
CDE-TT files, 94
character display console, 6
CHOOSER string
definition, 9
identifying, 9
client type control, 229
CLIENT_GEOMETRY field, 233
CLIENT_NAME field, 232, 233
clients
definition, 86
of server, configuring, 93
window in Front Panel, 233
client-server configuration, See networking
clock type control, 229
color
color sets, 266
controlling, with dynamicColor resource, 273
controlling, with Style Manager, 269
creating shades with shadowPixmaps resources, 272
maximum number allocated, 270
specifying foreground, 272
usage in icons, 209
color palettes, 265
color resources,modifying for registration, 59
color server, 25
resources, 30
starting, 30
color sets, 265, 266
default, 268
mapping to display elements, 267
colors
active window frame, 267
administering, 265
application windows, 267
colorsets, 266
default, 268
inactive window frame, 267
number used, 269
palettes, 265
resources, 266
text entry areas, 267
values, 267
colorUse resource, 31, 269, 271
COMMAND action, 156
example, 159
execution string, 166
required fields, 166
command line for actions, 166
command-line login, 5
configuration files
action, 157
data types, 187
Front Panel, 212
in registration package, 56
Login Manager, 21
Session Manager, 37
Window Manager, 242
Workspace Manager, 242
CONTAINER_NAME field, 217, 218, 222
CONTAINER_TYPE field, 217
CONTENT field, 193, 197
content-based data type, 149, 197
control

D

E

F

K

L

M

N

O

P

Q

R

readme files, 73
read-only data type criteria, 196
registration
  See also registration package
  actions needed, 62
  application group, 68
  application root directory, 60
  color modifications, 59
  data types needed, 62
  definition, 43, 57
  dtappintegrate, 75
  example, 77 to 83
  features provided by, 54
  font modifications, 59
  general steps, 57
  help files, 66
  icon requirements, 67
  modifying resources, 58
  overview, 54
  purpose of, 56
  resource modification, 58
registration package, 43
  See also registration
  application group contents, 72
  application icon, 72
  definition, 57
  directories, 60
  example of creating, 77
  Front Panel control, 74
  purpose of, 54
  readme files, 73
Reload Actions action, 161
Reload Applications action, 49
Reload Resources action, 30
remote execution
  by actions, 177
  configuring application server, 100
  native language support, 282
  with action remote from
    application, 104
RESOURCE_MANAGER property, 30, 33
resources
  app-defaults, 256
  colorUse, 271
  default desktop, 29
  display-specific, 33
  fonts, 261
  foregroundColor, 272
  language-dependent, 279
  loading, 29
  personal, 256
  session, 25
  setting, 33, 256
  shadow thickness of windows, 273
  shadowPixmaps, 272
  system-wide, 256
Restore Front Panel action, 215
RGB color value, 267
RGB values, 267
rgb.txt file, 267
root menu, See Workspace menu
root window, 246
rpc.cmsd, 99
rpc.ttdbserver, 95, 96

S

.sdl files, 66
search paths
  actions, 157
  applications, 41, 116
  current value, 115
  defined by desktop, 114
  environment variables, 115
  Front Panel definitions, 212
  help, 123
  icons, 204
  input variables, 114
  localized, 125
  output variables, 115
  set by Session Manager, 27
  setting, 115
secondaryColorSetId resource, 267, 269
selectColor resource, 267
Selected menu, 130, 136, 137
sendmail, 93
servers

X

THE COMMON DESKTOP ENVIRONMENT TECHNICAL LIBRARY

CDE DOCUMENTATION GROUP

Titles Available from Addison-Wesley

The Common Desktop Environment Technical Library is the official documentation for users, system administrators, and application developers of the graphical user interface that makes applications running on UNIX® systems portable and easy to use. Developed by IBM, Hewlett-Packard, SunSoft, and Novell, CDE has become the de facto standard in the UNIX marketplace because it unites different platforms under a single user interface.

Common Desktop Environment 1.0: User's Guide

Provides an easy-to-follow guide for getting the most out of the graphical user interface and its integrated productivity tools.

$24.75, paperback, 370 pages
ISBN 0-201-48951-1

Common Desktop Environment 1.0:
Advanced User's and System Administrator's Guide

Covers advanced tasks in customizing the appearance and behavior of the desktop. Many of the tasks require root permission.

$24.75, paperback, 320 pages
ISBN 0-201-48952-X

Common Desktop Environment 1.0:
Programmer's Overview

Introduces the CDE development environment and the developer documentation set.

$19.50, paperback, 112 pages
ISBN 0-201-48953-8

Common Desktop Environment 1.0: Programmer's Guide

Provides an in-depth exploration of the CDE development environment. Includes task-oriented descriptions of how to use each element, complete with code examples.

$24.75, paperback, 208 pages
ISBN 0-201-48954-6

Common Desktop Environment 1.0:
Help System Author's and Programmer's Guide

Covers how to develop on-line help for application software.

$34.50, paperback, 320 pages
ISBN 0-201-48955-4

Common Desktop Environment 1.0:
ToolTalk Messaging Overview

Introduces the ToolTalk service, a technology that allows developers to create applications that can interoperate with other applications.

$24.75, paperback, 176 pages
ISBN 0-201-48956-2

Common Desktop Environment 1.0:
Desktop KornShell User's Guide

For programmers who don't want to use C, shows how to create Motif applications with Desktop KornShell (dtksh) scripts.

$19.50, paperback, 128 pages
ISBN 0-201-48957-0

Common Desktop Environment 1.0:
Application Builder User's Guide

Explores Application Builder, a development tool that makes designing, creating, and prototyping a user interface easier.

$24.75, paperback, 176 pages
0-201-48958-9

ORDER INFORMATION

Available wherever computer books are sold or call Addison-Wesley directly at 1-800-822-6339 in the United States. You may send an order via fax to 1-800-367-7198. International Orders can be faxed to 1-617-942-2829.